Using Metaphors in Psychotherapy

Using Metaphors in Psychotherapy

By

PHILIP BARKER
MB, BS, FRCP(Ed), FRCPsych, FRCP(C), DPM, DCH

Professor of Psychiatry and Pediatrics, University of Calgary
Psychiatrist, Alberta Children's Hospital, Calgary

BRUNNER/MAZEL, *Publishers* • New York

Library of Congress Cataloging in Publication Data

Barker, Philip Alan.
  Using metaphors in psychotherapy.

  Bibliography: p. 213
  Includes index.
  1. Metaphor—Therapeutic use.   2. Psychotherapy.
I. Title.
RC489.M47B37   1985   616.89′14   85-15171
ISBN 0-87630-716-0 (pbk.)   ISBN 0-87630-410-2 (cloth)

Published by
BRUNNER/MAZEL, INC.
19 Union Square West
New York, New York 10003

MANUFACTURED IN THE UNITED STATES OF AMERICA

10 9 8 7

To Samantha, Karen, Jerome, and Clifton,
and their struggles to survive and grow.

Foreword

History abounds with accounts of people's attempts to improve their knowledge of themselves. Religious tracts like the Bible give straight directives (commandments), as well as illustrative examples (parables). Philosophers and theologians of all ages have carefully developed and argued their moral laws and principles, but we remember more readily, and with greater pleasure, the fables of poets like Aesop and La Fontaine. More recently, the behavioral sciences have offered new discoveries about human interaction that help us plan for the future, yet the average person of our time appears to pay more attention to the stories of a Hans Christian Andersen, a Walt Disney, or contemporary television soap operas.

Direct teaching of behavioral laws and principles often meets with resistance on the part of those being taught because the message is too direct, too personal, too shocking or, not infrequently, too difficult to understand. Soap operas, fables, and parables have the advantage that they tell us about ourselves in an indirect and thus more acceptable manner.

The many psychological therapies available today vary along several important dimensions. One of these is the manner in which new information is introduced. Some therapists are highly directive, like parents of young children; others are totally non-directive; and still others fall in between these extremes. The appropriateness of one or another approach depends in large measure on the learning abilities of the clients, not simply on the preference of the therapist. Clients' abilities are much influenced by age, social class, education, intelligence, and culture. The criteria of suitability for the traditional psychotherapies unfortunately are such that many potential clients find themselves without therapy.

The author of this book, leaning heavily on the work of Milton Erickson, describes in detail the use of metaphors in psychotherapy, with particular emphasis on the treatment of family groups. Most appropriately, too, the author relies heavily on the use of stories or metaphors as teaching devices, as the family therapist would rely on their use in the treatment of families.

The power of metaphors quite clearly lies in their ability to reach an affective component of the personality that, commonly, is too strongly defended to be reachable. This is the component that Bettelheim has described so well in his book on fairy tales, namely, the part of the person that wishes to discover new things but that at the same time is conscious of the need to protect the person against possible adverse results of such discoveries. This is why the use of metaphors and indirect approach is so essential in dealing with resistance.

This book will be of great help to many therapists and their clients.

S.K. Littmann, MB, ChB, FRCPsyh, FRCP(c), DPM
Professor and Head
Department of Psychiatry
University of Calgary

Contents

Introduction

The therapist's first session with the family was drawing to a close. The father, the mother, and the three children were all present.

The therapist recommended that the family come for subsequent sessions as a family group. The father, a foreman for a construction company, was working on a project in another part of the province and got home only on weekends. He said he couldn't make it during the therapist's working hours, though he could come late in the evening or at the weekend. It seemed that therapy would have little chance of success without the father's active involvement, but the therapist wasn't available in the evenings or on weekends. An impasse seemed to have been reached.

Then the therapist had an idea. Turning to the mother, he told her a story about how, when a hospital he had been associated with was under construction, the plumbers had gone on strike. The other trades, he explained, had tried to continue working. At first they thought they could achieve something without the presence of the plumbers. It wasn't long, though, before they found that whatever they did there was some little task that required the services of a plumber. So they got nowhere and achieved nothing. Not until the strike ended was any real progress made.

At that the father got out his appointment book and said, "Maybe I could get away early on a Friday every second or third week" and made an appointment suitable to the therapist.

* * *

Several decades ago, a group of men at the University of Wisconsin started a serious writers' group. Calling themselves "The Stranglers," they were merciless in criticism. Not to be outdone, a group of women, who named themselves "The Wranglers," set up a corresponding group. But their idea was to accentuate the positive, to look for the good in their colleagues' work, to be encouraging and gentle in their criticism.

Twenty years later, the university, curious as to what had happened to the two groups, made a survey. Each group had had equal talent; only their approach had differed. And what had happened? Not one of the men had amounted to anything as a writer. But of the women's group, half a dozen were notably successful. They were led by Marjorie Kinnan Rawlings, author of the classic novel, *The Yearling*.

* * *

Ann-Marie had been in hospital for investigation of fainting attacks, abdominal pain, and various other symptoms for which no physical cause was found. She lived alone with her mother; the two of them were very closely involved with each other and seemed to have been so since the unexpected sudden death of the father a year previously.

After Ann-Marie had been fully investigated in hospital and given a clean bill of physical health, she and her mother were referred for family therapy. This therapy focused on the tightly enmeshed relationship between Ann-Marie and her mother. Progress during the first three sessions was slow, but at the fourth the mother reported that on July 4th Ann-Marie's periods had started, and since then she had had none of her physical symptoms.

"Of course," replied the therapist. "It was Independence Day!"

A look of enlightenment came over the mother's face, as if she finally understood something she had been struggling with; at the same time a faint smile crossed her daughter's face.

After that Ann-Marie had no more symptoms.

The anecdotes above illustrate how meaning may be conveyed metaphorically; they may also have given you a flavor of the power of metaphorical communication. But how, you may ask, can I suddenly start talking about construction sites or writers' groups (to say nothing of jazz bands, computers, and tanker truck drivers, which are among the subjects mentioned later in the book) in the course of my therapy sessions? What will my clients think of me? Will they think I'm crazy—something many of them think about psychiatrists and other therapists anyway?

In fact, the use of metaphors is surprisingly easy, once rapport is established, and the right therapeutic atmosphere has come to exist; it *is* necessary, however, to set the scene by communicating indirectly—using anecdotes, analogies, similes, stories and examples from the start—so that your clients come to expect indirect communication. These issues are dealt with in Chapter 11, which tells you how to establish rapport with clients, so that they will listen to stories, learn from them, and carry out the tasks you set them.

In this book I have gathered together information from various sources on the use of metaphors in psychotherapy, as well as drawing on my own clinical experience. Most of the examples concern the treatment of common problems encountered in psychotherapeutic practice. I have used stories, and quoted examples (camouflaged to protect the identities of those concerned), to make important points throughout the book, for how else could such a book be written?

You can use metaphors whatever your area of psychotherapeutic practice. Metaphorical methods can be applied in virtually any clinical situation; the principles are the same.

In the following pages I set out my understanding of the principles underlying the therapeutic use of metaphors and illustrate them with examples. For those of you who cannot wait to practice on your own clients, I have included practical exercises at the end of each chapter except the first.

Philip Barker

Acknowledgments

Many colleagues have helped me with this book. Foremost among them is Karen Rempel, a gifted therapist and valued colleague on the staff of the Mental Health Program at Alberta Children's Hospital. Karen Rempel inspired me to write the book in the first place. She has contributed valuable material to it, notably that about Fay in Chapter 2, Brad the Brat in Chapter 7 and Trevor in Chapter 10, and she reviewed the manuscript and made many helpful suggestions.

Other colleagues who have reviewed drafts of the book are Evan Coppersmith, who also drew my attention to publications of hers in which highly creative use is made of metaphorical devices; Timothy Yates; and Sebastian Littmann. All have made valuable suggestions, as has Richard Crowley, that have been incorporated into the book. Joyce Mills drew my attention to Susan Lamb's UCLA thesis on hemispheric lateralization and storytelling, for which I am very grateful. My wife, Heather, read carefully through several drafts of the book and suggested many textual changes that I believe have made the book clearer and more readable.

I am grateful to Bernie Mazel, my publisher, for his enthusiastic support for the idea of a book on the use of metaphors in psychotherapy and to my editor, Ann Alhadeff, for her courtesy, patience, and efficiency.

The book would not have been the same without the help I have received from those I have named. Nevertheless, it remains my responsibility, along with the errors and imperfections that I am sure must exist.

Philip Barker

Using Metaphors
in Psychotherapy

1

Metaphor: A Time-Honored Way of Communicating

Anne was a bright and ordinarily happy 12-year-old who had, in the past, done well at school. Recently, however, her performance had dropped off, and she had lost interest particularly in her social studies class which she described as "boring." Her parents, naturally concerned, discussed the matter with other family members, including their own parents.

One day Anne was visiting her maternal grandmother, a wise woman and the mother of six successful adults. During their conversation Anne mentioned that she found her social studies class boring and wasn't doing well in it, something the grandmother had already heard about from Anne's parents. "Gran," as Anne called her, listened carefully to her granddaughter's account of her troubles at school but said little for the moment.

A week later Anne was at her grandmother's again.

"How are things at school?" asked Gran.

"The same," replied Anne laconically. "Miss Beaton's still behaving like an old cow. [Miss Beaton was Anne's

3

social studies teacher.] I hate her. She makes things so boring.''

"Would you like some ice cream?'' Gran asked. "I've got some of the kind you like." Gran knew that Anne had a particular liking for vanilla ice cream with chocolate chips in it and had bought some in anticipation of her visit.

Anne readily accepted her grandmother's offer, and Gran gave her a large helping of her favorite ice cream. And as Anne sat there eating Gran started to tell her a story.

"I once knew a boy,'' she said, "who lived at the seaside. This was when your mother was about your age and we lived in Devon. This boy—his name was Charles and he was about 13—came from a good family who cared a lot about him. On the whole he got along well with his parents, who thought he was a pretty good kid. But there was one problem between Charles and his parents. His parents liked to go for walks along the seashore; they did this almost every day and they expected Charles and his 9-year-old sister, Diane, to go with them. Diane still enjoyed the walks but Charles was starting to find them dull and boring. Whenever he could find an excuse to stay at home—like having a lot of homework to do—he did so, but he still ended up going on the walks most days.

"Then one day Charles, who was walking with his head hung down, well behind the others (to show his parents he was bored and in a sulk at having to be there), began to notice the seashells on the beach. He reached down and picked one up. It was quite small, reddish in color, and very pretty, Charles thought. As he walked, trailing behind his parents, he noticed other shells. There were shells of different shapes, sizes, and colors. Some were whole and in good shape, others were slightly damaged and incomplete, and still others were little more than broken fragments.

"By the time the family got home Charles had collected about a dozen shells of several different types. He took them to his room and examined them. He found himself wondering where they came from, what their names were and what kind of shellfish they had been.

"The next day Charles went to the school library and found a book on shellfish. He took it home and compared the shells he had with the pictures in the book. He was able to discover the names of about half of them. He knew now that he had to find a bigger book that contained more details about shells, so he asked his parents to take him to the public library. Here he found a much larger selection of books and picked out two that provided a lot more information than he'd found in the school library.

"Charles was now properly into shells and shellfish. He even became pleased when his parents asked him to go for walks along the shore, as this gave him opportunities to find more shells, or specimens in better shape. Over the next few months he became quite an expert on shellfish. He did a successful science project on them at school, entered the science fair, and won first prize in his class. And his walks along the seashore were no longer boring."

WHAT IS METAPHOR?

Collins Dictionary of the English Language (Hanks, 1979) defines a metaphor as "a figure of speech in which a word or phrase is applied to an object or action that it does not literally denote in order to imply a resemblance." This dictionary cites as an example the phrase "He is a lion in battle."

Turbayne (1970), in his book *The Myth of Metaphor*, prefers Aristotle's broader definition:

Metaphor consists in giving the thing a name that belongs to something else; the transference being either from genus to species or from species to species or on the grounds of analogy.

Turbayne advocates making Aristotle's definition wider still. Pointing out that metaphor need not be expressed in words, he suggests that Aristotle's "name" could mean a sign or collection of signs. Thus, Michelangelo used the figure of Leda with the swan to illustrate being lost in the rapture of physical passion, and the same figure of Leda, but without the swan, to illustrate being lost in the agony of dying. Similarly, blackboard diagrams, the toy blocks children use to represent battles, or the raised eyebrow of an actor may all be regarded as metaphorical expressions.

Turbayne (1970) concludes, following Aristotle's definition, that the model, the parable, the fable, the allegory, and the myth are all subclasses of metaphor. All can, of course, be taken literally. To the uninitiated, Michelangelo's Leda is just a feature of a painting, and Newton's concepts of "force" and "attraction" are literal truths. What Turbayne, a literary scholar and not a therapist, fails to consider is that a person may take a metaphor literally on the conscious level, while on the unconscious level perceiving its symbolic meaning. It is on this assumption that the clinical use of metaphorical communication is based.

The story Anne was told by her grandmother is an example of the use of metaphor. The grandmother started by establishing rapport with Anne (a process discussed further in Chapter 11); the metaphorical part starts with the paragraph beginning, "I once knew a boy. . . . " Charles represented Anne. The attitude he took while walking along the seashore was a metaphor for Anne's current attitude towards school, particularly her social studies classes. But then one day Charles discovered that there were, after all, interesting things about the seashore, namely the many varieties of seashells. What had been a dull and boring activity suddenly took on a new perspective. Some things he had formerly totally overlooked—the shells—proved to have great interest for him, and his growing interest in them, and its rewards, are described quite fully.

This story was designed to suggest, metaphorically, that there might be interesting things about social studies which Anne had hitherto overlooked. She had proved resistant to being told to work harder, and to explanations that what she was supposed to be studying *was* important and interesting, so Gran had the excellent (but of course not original) idea of conveying the points she wished to make metaphorically.

In the psychotherapy literature also the term "metaphor" has been given a broad meaning. Gordon's (1978) *Therapeutic Meta-*

phors, for example, is devoted largely to explaining how to construct and deliver long stories with metaphorical meanings in the course of psychotherapy. In addition, therapists sometimes use objects (as in the *metaphoric object* described by Angelo, 1981) and activities (Papp, 1980) that may have metaphorical meanings.

Metaphor has been an essential feature of human communication from time immemorial. Stories and anecdotes have long been used to convey specific messages; they are easy to apply in the course of psychotherapy. For this reason, they will be emphasized in this book, although several other metaphorical devices will also be discussed.

One of the earliest recorded stories is to be found in the Bible. The Book of Job, which appears in both Christian and Jewish scriptures and which probably dates back about 2500 years, is about God, the Devil and Job, a good and God-fearing man. The Devil challenges God to allow him to tempt Job to sin, hoping to get Job to abandon his trust in God. God accepts the challenge, subject to the condition that the Devil must spare Job's life.

Job subsequently experiences many kinds of personal disaster. He goes from a condition of great wealth to one of abject poverty, losing not only his material possessions but his family and his own personal health. In long discussions with three friends he agonizes: Should he abandon his faith in God, who has allowed this desperate situation to come about? Has God deserted him? What shall he do?

Like the best stories, the Book of Job is spun out to provide the maximum dramatic effect, but the outcome is that Job remains faithful to God and in the end is rewarded by even greater wealth and more sons and daughters than he had before.

Many people regard the Book of Job as a piece of fiction— divinely inspired fiction, perhaps, but not an account of actual events. They see it as a piece of Jewish folklore, written to illustrate a truth about God and his relationship to human beings.

Others, including many evangelical Christians, take it at its face value, believing it to be literally true.

For many people, the importance of the Book of Job, like that of much religious writing, lies in the message it carries. Those who argue over whether it is literally true may miss the point of the story—that God is ultimately in charge, that his will finally prevails, that those who believe in him will not be tempted beyond the limits they can withstand, and that faith in God has its eventual rewards. And what a compelling way of making these points! Much more persuasive than simply stating them, as we have just done.

Jesus taught in *parables*, stories powerful enough to have survived 2000 years. Characters from these stories, like the Good Samaritan and the Prodigal Son, have become part of our everyday vocabulary.

Greek mythology, like other mythologies, abounds with stories that are rich in symbolic meaning; the tale of Daedalus and Icarus is a good example.

> Daedalus, a prince of Athens, was a skilled craftsman, the work of his hands being the pride of the gods. He was an architect, a sculptor, a builder of ships, a carpenter, and also the first plumber. One day, while he and his son Icarus were visiting the Island of Crete, Daedalus helped his cousin, Theseus, escape death. Minos, King of Crete, intended to sacrifice Theseus to the Minotaur—a monster, half man, half bull—but Daedalus showed Theseus how to find his way out of the labyrinth in which the latter was confined. The king was furious and ordered Daedalus's arrest and imprisonment. Minos knew that even if Daedalus got out of the labyrinth he could not escape from the island, for all departing ships were searched.
>
> Daedalus concluded that, since the king controlled the land and the sea, the only avenue of escape open to him was the sky. He began to study birds and the structure of their wings. He set his son, Icarus, to trapping seagulls and plucking their feathers, and when there were enough feathers, Daedalus skillfully sewed them together and made four

wings that resembled those of giant birds. Using melted wax, he attached each wing to a wooden framework. Then he fastened one pair of wings to his own arms and the other to those of Icarus.

Day after day Daedalus and his impatient son, Icarus, practiced flying. Daedalus was a cautious man as well as a clever one and he did not want to embark on a flight across the sea until he and Icarus were skilled at flying and until their muscles were strong enough to last the journey.

At last the two men could fly with almost the same grace as birds. It was time to escape from Crete. Daedalus instructed his son as follows:

"You must steer a middle course," he said. "Don't fly too high or the sun may scorch your feathers or melt the wax of your wings. And don't fly too low or the mist from the sea will cling to your wings and make them too heavy for you to lift. I will lead and you must follow closely behind me until we get to the shores of Athens."

Daedalus and Icarus then rose gracefully into the air. At first Icarus followed closely behind his father, but as he grew more confident he went higher and higher. No man had ever been so high before. As Icarus got nearer and nearer to the sun, its hot rays melted the wax holding the feathers to his wings. As the feathers fell off, he started dropping down. He flapped his wings faster and faster, as his father had taught him, but there were no longer enough feathers to hold him up.

Icarus called to his father to save him, but there was nothing Daedalus could do. He could only watch his son plunge to his death in waters which have since been called the Icarian Sea.

This was the end of man's first attempt to fly. A heartbroken Daedalus flew on to Sicily, where he vowed never to fly again.

This story, even in this abbreviated form, is full of symbolic meaning. Quite apart from what it says about father–son and ruler–subject relationships, it teaches us the virtues of careful observation and diligent practice and the dangers of overconfidence. In these days when many young people like to get "high" on drugs, the story offers a metaphorical meaning related to the dangers of substance abuse. All these points could, of course, be made directly, but in metaphorical form they have more force and interest than would a series of injunctions about what one should and should not do. Made indirectly, moreover, the points are less likely to be resisted, and the chances of the storyteller being seen as moralistic are much reduced.

FAIRY TALES AND OTHER LITERATURE

Fairy tales and stories are important to most societies, though they go by different names in different cultures. Such narrative accounts tell listeners or readers about the human condition in particularly graphic ways. Long before the neglect, abuse, and exploitation of children became the subject of general discussion and debate, for example, the story of Cinderella said something about the mistreatment of stepchildren. Even the simple and sad tale of Humpty Dumpty carries its message: Be careful what you do because sometimes even the experts can't repair the damage resulting from ill-judged acts!

Bettelheim (1977) examines the use and value of fairy tales in his book *The Uses of Enchantment*. Such tales, Bettelheim maintains, are "a unique art form." The fairy tale not only entertains, it also enlightens children about themselves, fosters their personality development, offers them meaning on many different levels, and enriches their lives in a great variety of ways.

According to Bettelheim, children can learn more about human beings' inner problems and about adaptive solutions to their predicaments from folk fairy tales than from any other type of story they can comprehend. Fairy tales provide the moral education that children need, subtly and by implication only, conveying the advantages of moral behavior through stories that seem meaningful and right to the child. Fairy tales speak about the "severe inner pressures" within children in ways children unconsciously understand. Bettelheim says such stories "offer examples of both temporary and permanent solutions to pressing difficulties,'' without belittling the inner struggles that growing up entails. He goes on to explain:

> This is exactly the message that fairy tales get across to the child in manifold form: that a struggle against severe difficulties in life is unavoidable, is an intrinsic part of human existence—but that if one does not shy away, but steadfastly meets unexpected and often unjust hardships, one masters all obstacles and at the end emerges victorious. (Bettelheim, 1977, p. 8)

Bettelheim also points out that the figures in fairy tales are either conspicuously good or bad, virtuous or vile, industrious or lazy, stupid or clever. Such polarization, which is characteristic of the young child's own thinking, permits the child to understand easily the difference between two extremes. The stories are also so constructed that children identify with the good person rather than with the bad one: The good person is usually more appealing (the "handsome" prince, the "beautiful" princess) and generally triumphs over the bad one.

Bettelheim goes on to discuss a number of fairy stories and their value and meanings. His book is a useful source of information for anyone who wants to use fairy tales, or indeed any metaphors, therapeutically or in the regular bringing up of children. The first tale he mentions is from the *Arabian Nights*, "The Fisherman and the Jinny." This story describes how a poor fisherman casts his net into the sea four times, first catching a dead jackass, then a pitcher of sand and water, next a potsherd and broken glass, and finally a copper jar. As the fisherman opens the jar, a huge cloud emerges and materializes into a giant Jinni (or *genie*) which threatens to kill him, despite all his entreaties. But the fisherman quickly thinks up a way of saving himself. He taunts the huge Jinni by doubting aloud that it could ever have fitted into such a small pot. He thus induces the Jinni to return to the jar to prove that it can do this. The fisherman then quickly caps the jar and throws it back into the ocean.

The story also contains an account of how the Jinni's ferocity came about. During the first hundred years the Jinni spent in the bottle he said in his heart, "Whoso shall release me, him will I enrich for ever and ever." But the century went by and he was not released. So he then said, "Whoso shall release me, for him will I open the hoards of the earth." But still no one set him free, and four hundred years passed. Then he said to himself, "Whoso shall release me, for him will I fulfill three wishes." Finally, when after five hundred years he still was not released, he said to himself, "Whoso shall release me, him will I slay."

Bettelheim points out that the above sequence of feelings matches those of young children who have been "deserted" by their mothers or, presumably, fathers. At first they think about how happy they will be when their parents return. With the passage of time, however, the eager anticipation reaches a climax, fades, and is replaced by rage. The Jinni story thus contains a psychological truth for children who hear it. It is also rich in other meanings; for example, the story notes that the fisherman has children. Children can thus cast themselves in either of two roles—the fisherman who defeats the Jinni, or the child of one who defeats it.

There are several other important features of this story. The fisherman's three unsuccessful attempts before he nets the bottle demonstrate that we cannot expect always to achieve success at the first try, but must persist. Then the story shows that overcoming the magic of someone as powerful as the Jinni is not achieved without effort and cunning. Another significant point is the parallel between the fisherman's four efforts crowned by success, and the four steps in the development of the imprisoned Jinni's feelings culminating in rage. Bettelheim (1977) comments:

> This juxtaposes the maturity of the parent–fisherman and the immaturity of the Jinny, and addresses the crucial problem which early life presents to all of us: whether to be governed by our emotions or our rationality. To put the conflict into psychoanalytic terms, it symbolizes the difficult battle we all have to struggle with: should we give in to the pleasure principle, which drives us to gain immediate satis-

faction of our wants or to seek violent revenge for our frustrations, even on those who have nothing to do with them—or should we relinquish living by such impulses and settle for a life dominated by the reality principle, according to which we must be willing to accept many frustrations to gain lasting rewards. (p. 33)

In contemporary culture the fairy tale seems to be losing ground to television programs and films. Interestingly, however, examination reveals that TV and film tend to have many of the features of the traditional fairy story. The "Star Wars" and "James Bond" films, for example, present the same conflict between good and evil, the same combination of magic and resourcefulness with which the heroes overcome their foes, and the same ultimate triumph of good over evil that fairy tales have long offered. Television series share similar characteristics. It may be, therefore, that these are the modern fairy tales that serve purposes similar to those served by the tales of the *Arabian Nights* and of the Brothers Grimm.

Television seems to have taken over the role of storyteller, though parents are still sometimes available to discuss with their children the stories seen on television. Having these contemporary fairy tales available on videocassettes, as increasingly they are, provides today's children with the opportunity to replay all or parts of them at will, rather as children of an earlier time used to ask their parents to read the same stories again and again.

Important as fairy tales are in the bringing up of children, and despite the fact that they can also be useful during psychotherapy, there is a very significant difference between their traditional use in families and their therapeutic use. Fairy tales, like many proverbs and biblical parables, usually make rather specific points and aim to teach specific lessons; therapeutic metaphors, on the other hand, offer new choices, especially new ways of looking at things, and can tap a variety of experiences, beliefs, and ideas that have been dormant in the listener's mind. Bettelheim (1977) insists on the importance of the repetition of the messages conveyed in fairy tales. The same probably applies to the use of

metaphors in psychotherapy; it can often be helpful to offer the
same message repeatedly in a series of metaphors.

Novelists also use metaphor extensively. Indeed some novels
are but extended metaphors. For example, when George Orwell
wanted to write about communism as a system, rather than make
a direct statement, he chose to create his now-famous novel *Animal
Farm* (1945). Poets and songwriters also tend to express their
meanings metaphorically. Jean de la Fontaine, the 17th-century
French poet, not only wrote many fables of his own but adapted
fables written in ancient times. These are delightful stories of
animals and nature, and La Fontaine uses them to make points
about the character and behavior of human beings. The poet's
tales tend to be somewhat moralistic, however, and are therefore
probably more useful as aids to childrearing than as metaphors
for use in psychotherapy. The same can be said for most of
Aesop's fables.

Songwriter Junior Parker had something to say about the human condition in the song *Mystery Train*, made famous by Elvis
Presley. The "long black train carry my baby from home," the
song goes, the train symbolizing all the things that can break up
a relationship with a loved one. The lyrics of blues singers also
abound with symbolism and metaphor. In the days when it was
not too safe to protest about the status of the black person in
America, the subject was often referred to metaphorically. Sexual subjects, too, were referred to in this way. One of the best
known songs of the late Lizzie Douglas (better known as "Mem-
phis Minnie") went as follows:

> Want to see my chauffeur, want to see my chauffeur,
> I want him to drive me, I want him to drive me down town,
> Says he drives so easy I can't turn him down.
>
> Well I must buy him, well I must buy him,
> A brand new V-8, a brand new V-8 Ford,
> Then he won't need no passengers, I will be his load.
>
> Gwine t'let my chauffeur, gwine t'let my chauffeur,

Drive me around the, drive me around the world,
Then he can be my li'l boy, yes an' I can be his girl.

The singer is not, of course, really singing about a chauffeur or a trip in a car.

Paul Oliver, a leading authority on the blues, refers repeatedly to the blues singer's use of metaphor. He notes, for example:

Not unnaturally the rhythms of love lead to many effective parallels which are made with the lusty bawdiness of an Elizabethan playwright, but in terms that are eminently of the present: the work of the automechanic, the oil driller or the steamboat captain alike become the themes of songs, neither wholly innocent nor shamefacedly secretive. (Oliver, 1963, p. 122)

ANECDOTES

Points can often be made by the use of quite short anecdotes. The following is an example of the sort of brief allusion that, in order to make a point, one can sometimes helpfully bring into the conversation during a therapy session.

I had a daughter who for several years had dreamed and talked about becoming a great saxophone player. The only problem was that she couldn't summon up enough enthusiasm to practice. And the more we bugged her to practice the less she did. In the end we decided to leave her to it. It was only when she went to the Stage Band festival, where she saw and heard a young girl taking really great solos in front of a high school band, that she became inspired to practice.

This anecdote makes several points quite briefly. First, by sharing a personal experience with the clients the therapist says, in effect, "Yes, bringing up children isn't easy—I've had my own frustrations—but this is how things worked out for us." The anecdote also suggests that to achieve something we often have to work hard at it; that bugging people to do things may produce an outcome that is opposite to what we wish to achieve; and that people can be inspired to work hard by seeing or hearing someone who has achieved what they themselves want to accomplish.

It is not always necessary to tell a long, involved story to make a point. Everyday conversation abounds with phrases like, "That reminds me of. . . . ," "I remember when. . . . ," "It's rather like. . . . ," "It's the same kind of situation as. . . . ," and so forth. Such phrases may introduce similes, rather than metaphors, but these too have therapeutic uses, and they are helpful in day-to-day communication. The main difference between a simile and a metaphor is that in the former the object or event does in some way directly resemble the object or situation with which it is compared, as in the phrase "he swims like a fish."

Proverbs, which are brief, metaphorical but somewhat didactic statements, can occasionally be used to make points during psychotherapy. "People in glass houses shouldn't throw stones," "Too many cooks spoil the broth," "A rolling stone gathers no moss," and "The grass is always greener on the other side of the fence" all make points in simple but oblique and often effective ways. Many proverbs, however, have become clichés, and therapists will usually do better to compose their own brief statements, tailored to the needs of their current clients.

In some situations, a remark as brief as the following might be useful: "I knew a man went into a hardware store and asked the storekeeper whether he should buy something." This anecdote may sound rather silly, but it may be helpful to people who come to the therapist asking whether they should undergo psychotherapy. It may help them consider whether they want to make any changes in their lives, relationships, emotional reactions, or behavior, just as the man in the hardware store needed to consider whether he had a use for any of the things the storekeeper had to sell and, if so, whether the time, trouble, and expense of buying and using them was worthwhile.

WHY ARE STORIES AND OTHER METAPHORS SO USEFUL?

Inasmuch as the use of metaphor as a means of communication has been widespread throughout recorded history, we must assume that there are distinct advantages to delivering messages in metaphorical form rather than in more direct ways. All forms of metaphor have similar advantages, but in discussing these we will use the example of stories, partly for simplicity's sake, but also because stories are probably the most used and one of the easiest ways of communicating metaphorically. In the following paragraphs we will discuss the main reasons for the value of the story as an elegant way of communicating. The reader should note that similar considerations apply to poetry, anecdotes, and tasks and activities with metaphorical meaning.

First, stories, if properly constructed and told, are usually more interesting than straight expositions of the points one wishes to make. Of course it is possible to construct boring stories or to tell good stories in a boring way. But well-thought-out and well-narrated stories, told in the right contexts, can capture the imagination, and inspire people to undertake tasks or think about things they would not have considered before. Such stories have the potential to bring people to the sudden realization of things, and they can also contribute to a more gradual learning process.

Those to whom stories are told (or tasks are given) can use their content in their own ways and can take from them those meanings that apply in their own particular situations. This is important when stories are used in the course of psychotherapy. Unlike fairy tales which, as we have seen, are mostly designed to put over quite specific points, therapeutic metaphors can readily be constructed to offer choice. It is often helpful to do this because psychotherapy is essentially a process of providing people with more choice in the matter of how they behave, or respond emotionally, in various situations.

Psychotherapy is seldom simply telling people what to do. It is more a matter of helping people to see things differently and to feel differently about them. Therapeutic metaphors, therefore, seldom need to be designed to convey specific injunctions. They are not usually necessary to put over an idea didactically.

A second important point is that stories, because they deal indirectly with issues and have meanings that are in varying degrees veiled, tend to be less threatening and confronting than direct statements. Not all the statements people make to each other are threatening, of course, and indeed most statements *are* made in direct, rather than story, form. But stories can make points gently. Listeners are free to take stories at their face value, if their implicit meaning (at least at the time) is unacceptable to them on a conscious level.

Related to the preceding notion is a third point: people can use stories in their own way and for their own purposes. The subject is given the opportunity to use the various meanings contained in the metaphor, at an unconscious level, in his or her own idiosyncratic way. Stories resemble projective tests, insofar as the latter mean different things to different subjects. Indeed it can sometimes be helpful to use vague metaphors, so that clients will draw on their own resources to fill in the gaps.

Even when a story is quite straightforward, as was the tale Anne's grandmother told her, any deeper meaning it may have will depend on the listener's current attitudes and state of mind. In this situation, unconscious factors—that is, processes of which the subject is not consciously aware—may be important. Anne could have taken many meanings from her grandmother's story, or it might have had little impact on her beyond its immediate interest and entertainment value. Yet the story did offer some clues as to how Anne might find something of interest in the school subject she experienced as dull. It was thus a promising alternative to simple exhortations to work harder, or suggestions that surely there must be something interesting in social studies.

The therapist, of course, can never be sure whether or how the client's unconscious will use a story or other metaphor. If a story is simply taken at face value, nothing is lost. On the other hand, if the therapist's points are made directly, there is a chance that the client will, quite consciously, reject them; this result could damage the existing therapist–client rapport. It is most important, especially when strategic therapy methods are used, that good rapport be maintained; communicating metaphorically can help achieve this goal. Thus if Anne had simply taken her grandmother's story at face value, and its potential metaphorical meaning had been lost on her at even the unconscious level, she might still have enjoyed it. In this case, her relationship with her grandmother would have remained untarnished, and the possibility of her grandmother helping her in other ways would not have been compromised, as it might have been had the grandmother lectured Anne on what she should be doing at school.

A fourth point, which will be discussed further later, is that some stories can directly affect a person's unconscious mind and attitudes. In this way one can evade the possibility that a rational point of view presented to a person may later be overruled by the person's feelings and unconscious attitudes.

A fifth point about stories is that they are flexible and can be used as a channel for many sorts of communication. While they can suggest solutions to problems, they can also present opinions—several different ones in one story if need be—impart information, give instructions or suggestions for action, and enable listeners to see things in new and different ways. This latter process is sometimes referred to as "reframing" and will be discussed in later chapters.

A sixth use of stories is that they enable one to say something to or about the person being addressed, but "in quotes." For example, one can have one character in a story say to another, "That was a foolish decision." The person to whom the story is being told is not directly threatened by this remark. Yet statements made in this way, if embedded appropriately in a story and delivered so that the embedded message is highlighted by being spoken in a different voice tone or at a different speed of talking, can have considerable impact on the listener. And again, if they do not, little or nothing has been lost.

A seventh point is that stories can be valuable in establishing rapport with people, especially children. In many cultures the telling or reading of stories to children is a common practice. The process can be, indeed should be, fun for both the storyteller and the listener. In contexts in which storytelling regularly occurs it will be a lot easier to include, along with other tales, stories with special meanings, told for particular purposes, than it will be in other settings. In the case of Anne and her grandmother there was a long history of storytelling. Gran was a great talker. While some people thought she talked too much, Anne, who was very fond of her, usually listened to her with rapt attention.

The relationship aspects of storytelling are exceedingly important. Effecting major changes in clients' psychological states is seldom easy and usually taxes the therapeutic relationship to the fullest. This applies with particular force when brief and strategic therapy methods are used. The telling of stories, however, does not threaten the therapeutic relationship and may actually strengthen it. Interpretations can also be offered metaphorically, if making them directly might be too threatening or might lead to their rejection.

Finally, stories and anecdotes offer an eighth advantage: they model a way of communicating. Growing up in a culture in which stories are regularly used to make points, present arguments, entertain, inform, persuade, provoke thought, and stimulate laughter gives people a model of this effective way of communicating. Among psychotherapists, the greatest storyteller was probably the late Milton Erickson. He used stories and "teaching tales" to great effect. In his writings and his teaching seminars, however, he rarely advocated specific use of these devices. Instead he suggested this approach to his students by modeling it. He usually answered questions from his students with anecdotes or longer stories, rather than directly (Erickson, 1980e). It seems that, especially toward the end of his life, he used the telling of stories as one of his main therapeutic approaches.

NEUROLOGICAL CONSIDERATIONS

All of the foregoing reasons for the widespread use of metaphor in human communication are essentially pragmatic; over the course of human history people have found that metaphor works. Recently, evidence has emerged of a neurological basis for the effectiveness of metaphor. According to Watzlawick (1978), metaphor is the language of the right cerebral hemisphere. And it seems that psychotherapy, if it is to lead to substantial change, has to address "right-brain" processes. What clients usually need is not a better logical understanding of their situation, but different emotional attitudes and different ways of interpreting the world around them.

Insight—the logical understanding of a situation—is of little value in itself. Understanding *why* you are behaving, or feeling, in a particular way does not usually help you to behave or feel differently. Even in psychoanalysis, interpretations are effective only when offered in the context of the transference relationship. It seems that in order to resolve a person's emotional or behavioral problems, what needs to change is the way the right cerebral hemisphere processes input.

It is probably an oversimplification to say simply that the left brain processes literal, sequential, and logical aspects of language, while the right brain processes the metaphorical aspects. Nevertheless, it does seem that there is some such division of work between the two hemispheres. And if this particular division does obtain, psychoanalysis addresses itself primarily to the left brain. This may explain why it tends to produce its results slowly; presumably it influences the right brain only indirectly. On the other hand, therapy methods that address the right brain directly—such as the use of stories, other forms of metaphor, embedded statements, and many hypnotherapy techniques—seem to produce results more quickly.

Lamb (1980) has reviewed the relationship of hemispheric specialization and storytelling. She points out that the idea that human beings have two ways of thinking has a long history, listing the many contrasting terms different scholars have used to label the two ways of thinking. Interestingly, all these dual sets of terms resemble those put forward by Watzlawick (1978) who explains:

> There are thus two languages involved. The one, in which for instance this sentence itself is expressed, is objective, definitional, cerebral, logical, analytic; it is the language of

reason, of science, explanation and interpretation, and therefore the language of most psychotherapy. The other . . . is
much more difficult to define—precisely because it is not the
language of definition. We might call it the language of
imagery, of metaphor, or *pars pro toto*, perhaps of symbols,
but certainly of synthesis and totality, and not of analytical
dissection. (pp. 14–15)

We might add that the latter language ("right brain language")
also includes poetry and nonverbal language as expressed in
facial expressions, voice tone, body postures, and movements
and dance.

In addition, Ornstein (1978) notes that "the brain's hemispheres
are not specialized for different types of materials (verbal and
spatial) but for different kinds of thought" (p. 82).

Lamb summarizes the situation as follows:

Recent research in neurology indicates that the two cerebral
hemispheres of the human brain process information by two
different strategies. The left hemisphere processes data in
a sequential, one-at-a-time fashion. Logical, temporal, verbal,
and analytic concerns are best handled by this hemisphere.
The right hemisphere processes information in a simultane-
ous, holistic fashion. Spatial, structural, kinesthetic, *gestalt*,
and metaphoric considerations are best handled by the right
hemisphere. The hemispheres communicate through the
corpus callosum. . . . In the functioning of a normal individual, hemispheric specialization is not an either/or propo-
sition; the bicameral brain works as a whole with one hemisphere dominating, depending on the nature of the task and
the preference of the individual. (Lamb, 1980, pp. 18–19)

Experimental evidence for the different functions of the two
hemispheres has come from electroencephalographic (EEG) studies of a group of bilingual Hopi Indian children (Rogers et al.,
1977). These children were told the same two stories in both
English and Hopi, and it was found that they evidenced greater
right hemisphere activity when Hopi was used than when English

was used. Hopi, a Native American language, is concerned with the immediately perceivable and links speech to its context; it is much less concerned than English with time and readily allows for timelessness. Hopi is concerned with the domain of nature, not with logic and abstract ideas. English, by contrast, is considered by Rogers and her colleagues to "orient its users to separation or abstraction from the perceptual field, leading to a concern with culture, to a context-free universe of discourse." The different EEG patterns observed in this study offer support for the idea of hemispheric specialization just outlined. (See also Chapter 11, where of the role of hypnosis in delivering metaphors is discussed.)

WHAT HAPPENED TO ANNE?

During the months following the talk with her grandmother recounted earlier, Anne made better progress in school, and she seemed a little happier. At the end of the year her grades were better than expected and she got a passing mark in social studies, which at one point her teachers had not thought she would do.

It is impossible to know, of course, whether and to what extent Anne's improvement was related to her discussions with her grandmother. Would she have improved anyway? Was she perhaps just going through a difficult period of adjustment to adolescence? The same questions arise when we try to evaluate the effects of psychotherapy; only a rigorously controlled trial could determine whether or not a particular therapeutic device or maneuver has a particular effect, and the difficulties involved in such a trial would be immense.

The foregoing does not of course absolve us from putting forth our best efforts in trying to help people with their problems. The story Gran told Anne certainly carried a message; indeed it carried several messages. What use Anne's unconscious made of these messages—or exactly what went on in her right cerebral hemisphere—we cannot know for certain, but the messages surely had the potential to help. In the final analysis, all any therapist

can do is offer help. The drowning man always has the option
to decide whether or not to grab the rope thrown to him by the
lifeguard.

SUMMARY

Various metaphorical devices have long been used by people
to communicate ideas. Stories, anecdotes and "teaching tales"
are examples of these devices, but actions and concrete objects
can also have metaphorical meanings, as will become clearer in
later chapters. All these devices offer advantages over the direct
and unadorned expression of opinions, points of view, injunctions, suggestions, insights, and even sometimes factual information. They can entertain as well as inform. They can suggest
things without confronting those to whom they are addressed.
They are indirect and often ambiguous and so can have various
meanings at different levels. They are flexible and can be used
to embed messages. They often assist in the establishment of rapport. They tend to be much used by effective communicators and
can be useful in the course of psychotherapy.

2

The Place of Metaphor in Psychotherapy

AN ABSENT FATHER

All five members of the Evans family had attended the preceding four family therapy sessions. They had originally sought help because John, 14, the oldest of the three children, had developed some rather severe behavioral problems. John's behavior had now improved greatly and he was back in school; the concern of the family had lessened considerably. Today, for the fifth session, the father was absent.

The therapist's earlier assessment had suggested that Mr. Evans had always been a somewhat peripheral figure within the family. He appeared to have been rather uninvolved emotionally with the other family members, busying himself with his work and leaving the care of the children and the home to his wife. When John developed his problems, the father became temporarily more involved with the family, but the therapist hypothesized that things were now slipping back to their former pattern.

On discovering that Mr. Evans was absent and learning from his wife that he had said he felt no need to attend further sessions, particularly since he was very busy in his furniture moving business, the therapist decided to address the matter of the father's absence at the start of the session.

The question was how to do this. It didn't seem a good idea to criticize the father, either explicitly or implicitly. Any such criticism would almost certainly have found its way back to Mr. Evans by way of at least one of the family members. Nor did it seem a good idea to blame the other members of the family, though the therapist did get the impression that the father did not feel much warmth or caring from them. So the following approach was adopted.

At the start of the session the therapist asked all the four members present, in turn, what they thought the therapist might have done in the last session, or the preceding ones, that had contributed to Mr. Evans' non-attendance today. Had he said something tactless to him? Had he made him feel left out of the discussion? Had he shown him insufficient care and concern? Not enough warmth and acceptance, perhaps? Did the father feel in some way blamed for the family's problems? How could the therapist have made him feel more a part of the therapy process? How did the therapist manage to leave Mr. Evans, apparently, with the idea that treatment could proceed satisfactorily without him? What could the therapist do now that would help the father once again to become part of the therapy process?

The above questions were all good ones in their own right; the therapist might indeed have done or said things that played a part in Mr. Evans' decision not to come to the session. But each question also had a metaphorical meaning. Every time a family member was asked a question about what the therapist might have said or done, or failed to do, that person was given an opportunity to think about what might have upset Mr. Evans and caused him to withdraw from the sessions and, perhaps, from other family situations. Almost inevitably the other family members would find themselves thinking about things *they* might have done or said to Mr. Evans that could have upset him or played a part in causing him to withdraw from the family.

The therapist's discussion of the father's absence from the session, framed largely in the form of questions, was thus a metaphorical way of considering Mr. Evans's absence from many of the family's activities. It was possible, of course, that the family would not take the questions in this way, even at the unconscious level, but if they did not, nothing would be lost. In that case some questions would have been asked and answered, but the matter of the father's withdrawal would not have been addressed at that particular time. And the damage that might have been done by implying, in some more direct way, that the other family members were partially responsible for Mr. Evans's absence was certainly avoided.

METAPHORS AND PSYCHOTHERAPY

The literature on the use of metaphors in psychotherapy is sparse, and hard research data are in short supply. Indeed, the latter scarcely exist at all, presumably because a controlled study of the use of metaphors would be exceedingly difficult to do. Yet the use of stories, anecdotes, rituals, and activities with a metaphorical content is widespread. Human beings regularly use metaphor to communicate with each other, so it is reasonable to expect this figure of speech to have a place in the process of communication we call psychotherapy.

Among therapists whose use of metaphor has been described in the literature, pride of place must go to Milton Erickson. *My Voice Will Go With You*, a compilation of Erickson's "teaching tales" edited by Sidney Rosen (1982), comprises 117 stories, mostly quite short, that Erickson used in treating his patients, teaching his students, or both. The book is a rich source of material for anyone who wants to use stories with a metaphorical meaning psychotherapeutically. Rosen adds his own brief comments on the stories, which are helpful without being intrusive. *A Teaching Seminar With Milton Erickson* (Erickson, 1980e), edited by Jeffrey Zeig, is a record of a week-long seminar given by Erickson in 1979, the year before his death. This book, too, contains mainly stories. When making a point, answering a question, or indeed teaching anything Erickson almost invariably used anecdotes or stories. Both these books well repay careful study by anyone interested in this method of communication.

Therapeutic Metaphors (Gordon, 1978) deals specifically with the construction and delivery of metaphors; indeed, after some general discussion of how to construct metaphors, the main part of the book consists of a detailed and rather lengthy description of the development of a specific story with a carefully designed metaphorical content that is intended to meet the needs of a particular clinical case. Unlike *My Voice Will Go With You*—which can be read purely for pleasure as well as for important therapeutic ideas—*Therapeutic Metaphors* is not easy reading. The latter book's ideas are sound, however, and it has much to offer the reader wanting to use full-length metaphorical stories in psychotherapy.

The Answer Within (Lankton & Lankton, 1983) is a book on Ericksonian hypnotherapy by two of Erickson's former students. It provides an in-depth account of the use of Erickson's *multiple embedded metaphors* technique in the course of hypnotherapy; this technique is discussed in Chapter 11. This is a learned and important book and a valuable source of information about metaphors; it is not, however, a book for the beginner.

THE CLINICAL USE OF ANECDOTES AND STORIES

In practice, anecdotes used clinically nearly always have a metaphorical content; that is, they are not directly concerned with the clinical situation under consideration but relate to it in some metaphorical way. Anecdotes differ from full-dress metaphors chiefly in being shorter and more circumscribed in their content and purpose and in not necessarily comprising a complete scenario, with characters and events to represent all the important ones in a real-life situation. Zeig (1980), in a helpful introduction to Erickson's *Teaching Seminar*, lists some of the ways Erickson used anecdotes.

Making or illustrating points. The stories that have appeared so far in this book all do this in one way or another. The story of Job, for example, made a number of important points. Had they been stated in essay form, these points would probably have sounded like a series of moralistic pronouncements, which many people would reject. But presented in story form—especially in a story about someone living in a different context and, here, a different time—they do not threaten the listener. Metaphors are part of the "language of change," described by Watzlawick (1978) and mentioned in the previous chapter. This is the "right brain" language of which poetry, drama, nonverbal language, as well as metaphor, are examples. It is the language of imagery, as distinct from "left brain" language, which expresses factual material in logical, well-defined ways, using an ordered pattern of syntactic rules.

Suggesting solutions to problems. In our Chapter 1 story, the grandmother could simply have told Anne that there must be something interesting about social studies and that she should make an effort to discover it. Or, like Anne's parents, she might have exhorted Anne to work harder. Instead she intuitively felt that the more indirect approach of telling a story might be effective where other approaches had failed.

Helping people to recognize themselves. People can sometimes be helped to recognize aspects of their behavior in or reactions to situations by being told about other people who behaved similarly in analogous situations. Consider, again, the story of Anne. The grandmother described how Charles, an adolescent of about Anne's age, walked with his head hung down, trailing some way behind his parents. This was an accurate description, in metaphorical form, of Anne's own attitude.

Seeding ideas and increasing motivation. An obvious way of increasing the motivation of poorly motivated clients, and of encouraging those who do not believe they can overcome their problems, is to tell such clients stories about people who have overcome similar problems. But any idea a therapist wants a client to consider or accept can be seeded in a series of anecdotes. For example the story of the young girl who learned to practice the saxophone (Chapter 1) could be used in a series of anecdotes suggesting that a client learn to practice something.

Controlling the therapeutic relationship. It is important that the therapist be in control of the therapeutic relationship. When clients challenge this control, one way of attaining and maintaining it is to tell the clients stories. This seems to work in part because psychotherapy clients do not normally expect to be told stories and are thus caught off guard. And the unexpected can be a powerful precipitator of change in therapy. In dealing with "resistant" families—those the therapist finds it difficult to help make changes—introducing something unexpected may suddenly free up the treatment process.

In the following example the family presented stating that "everything" that might solve their problem had been tried but had failed. It was necessary for the therapist to take control of the session, rather than let it continue along the lines upon which the family had set it. In this case, metaphorical devices other than stories were used.

> The Young family had consulted several therapists over the preceding four years, but the severe temper tantrums of their 8-year-old son, William, had intensified. William would break windows, tear shelves off walls, and kick holes in doors. Well-qualified professionals had given the parents a good deal of sound advice about dealing with tantrums, but when the Youngs tried to put it into practice, none of it had worked. It would take a miracle, Mr. and Mrs. Young said, to cure the tantrums. I got the impression that the Youngs did not think I was a miracle worker.
>
> Obviously, more advice on how to deal with tantrums would not suffice. Once the assessment of the family had been completed, something new and different from what had been offered them previously was needed. Advice, anecdotes, interpretations, and reframings had apparently all been tried, but *paradoxical injunctions* had not.
>
> I then told the family I needed to know more about the tantrums, which were clearly something out of the ordinary. Before recommending any treatment I would like to see one. So I asked William to have a tantrum there in the therapy

room. William appeared surprised and said that, though he could have one if he wished, he didn't feel like it at that moment. My attempts to persuade him were unsuccessful.

For a short while I did my best to appear at a loss as to what to do. Then I told the parents I had an idea.

"Do you have a cassette recorder at home?" I inquired.

"Yes," they said.

"Would you be prepared to have it ready at all times, with a cassette loaded in it, so that you could record one or two of William's tantrums for me, and bring the recording to the next session?" I asked.

"Yes, we could do that," Mr. Young replied, also apparently a little surprised.

I explained that it would help me a lot to hear a tantrum and told William to be sure that his next one was a good one and that he shouted really loud so that everything could be heard clearly on the tape. William looked puzzled. Then he asked a question.

"What happens if I don't have a tantrum before the next appointment with you?"

"You *must* have one," I told him. "If you don't we'll never get anywhere with the treatment of your problem."

When the parents expressed a similar concern, I set the next appointment for six weeks hence. This should leave time, I said, for many tantrums, for William had several in a typical week. I also said that if, by any chance, they had not got a good recording of a tantrum by the day before the next appointment they could call in and postpone it. And they did just that!

I did not myself speak to Mrs. Young when she called. I waited three weeks before doing anything else about the family. Then I telephoned the family and spoke to Mrs. Young, who said that she and her husband just couldn't understand it but William had had no more tantrums. Moreover, he didn't want to return to the hospital to see me and the parents couldn't see any point in it either, now that the tantrums were no longer occurring. I agreed with this conclusion but suggested they keep the tape recorder ready—just in case.

ıse vignette illustrates the use of four strategic devices:
pected; a paradoxical injunction (see also Barker, 1981a); a relauoship metaphor; and a metaphorical object, the cassette recorder. (It also illustrates the point that several types of strategic intervention, of which metaphor may be one, can be used simultaneously.)

In the past, all the Youngs' attempts to prevent William from having tantrums had failed, and the more they tried to stop the tantrums the worse the latter got. William was a negativistic child; he denied almost everything that was said about him in the session and was generally uncooperative and hostile. His reaction to my *paradoxical injunction*—telling him that he *must* have a tantrum before the next session—was predictable. But the interaction between William and the therapist was also a *relationship metaphor*—a metaphor for the relations between him and his parents. It offered the parents an understanding, which probably remained unconscious, of the fact that William tended to do the opposite of what he was told, thus becoming the center of attention.

For William, after the therapy session described, being oppositional involved *avoiding* having tantrums, and the loaded cassette recorder remained as a *metaphorical object*—a metaphor for me, the therapist, whom he did not wish to see! The parents, for their part, could now choose to turn the psychological tables on William at home, much as I had done in my meeting with the family.

Control issues frequently have to be addressed in therapy, whether the problem is that of having the therapist, rather than the client in control of the sessions, or whether it is a matter of having parents gain control of rebellious or oppositional children. Useful in dealing with control issues might be a story about a plane that crashed because the pilot was fighting with a passenger or, less dramatic and alarming, a story about a ship that sailed off course because the captain was arguing with the mate. Or stories could be told about business enterprises or military units that failed because of lack of direction and control.

Embedding directives. Directives to clients can be embedded in stories. This technique, of saying things "in quotes," was mentioned in Chapter 1.

Decreasing resistance.   Because anecdotes present ideas indirectly and, often, a little at a time, they are less likely to be resisted than are ideas presented more directly. Anecdotal messages, because of their structure, can become unconscious quickly. The patient cannot consciously absorb and understand all of the messages contained in a complex anecdote. The patient can experience a behavior change occurring outside of his or her conscious awareness because he or she can respond to part of an anecdote even though that part was not registered consciously.

Reframing and redefining problems.   Reframing and redefining are at the heart of the psychotherapy process, for if the subject does not emerge from therapy with a different view of things—at least of some things—there has been no real change. The reframing may of course be at the unconscious level—indeed ideally it usually is—but it must occur if the client is to emerge truly changed.

Ego-building.   Subjects who have difficulty dealing effectively with the real world around them can be told stories about how other people have learned to do so, especially people who share some personality characteristics with the subject.

Modeling a way of communicating.   Story-telling as a model of communication was mentioned in Chapter 1. Milton Erickson once said that if you want a man to tell you about his brother, you should tell him about yours.

Reminding subjects of their own resources.   Erickson believed that his patients had the resources in their own histories to resolve their problems. He often used stories to remind people that they had learned many useful things in the past and had perhaps simply forgotten them.

Desensitizing people from their fears.   By telling phobic clients a series of anecdotes dealing with their particular phobic objects or situations, while being careful not to raise their level of tension too high, it is possible to reduce or eliminate fears. This technique resembles part of the process of systematic desensitization.

The reader will have noticed that the metaphorical statements in the story at the beginning of this chapter were contained not in anecdotes but in questions. As we saw in Chapter 1, many things can have metaphorical significance and can be used in therapy. Thus a series of interactions between therapist and client or family may constitute a metaphor for the interactions among family members or between the family and people outside the family circle. Tasks carried out during therapy sessions or between them may also have metaphorical meaning.

> Fay had lived in a common-law relationship with George for 18 months. The relationship was a stormy one, and Fay was highly ambivalent about it. When Fay eventually decided to leave George, she and her two sons of a previous marriage nevertheless mourned his loss. Fay complained that she couldn't sleep at night, thought constantly about George, was unable to concentrate, and felt lonely. At interview she also appeared moderately depressed. It seemed important that she discard the unhappy associations and memories, as she came to terms with the separation. Had she not resolved her feelings she might have been tempted to seek a reconciliation with George, as she had done with men she had lived with before.
>
> Fay still had a number of items in her house that reminded her of George. Some things had belonged to him, others he had left behind, and still others were his gifts to Fay.
>
> After exploring Fay's feelings and situation carefully with her, the therapist gave her the following task. She was to go through everything in the house that had belonged to George and decide whether it was worth keeping or whether it was something that would be better got rid of. The two

classes of things were to be placed in different boxes. Fay was then to take the box of things that were not worth keeping, make a fire in the backyard, and burn the box and its contents. As she did so, she was to weep as much as she felt like doing.

The other box now contained all those things of George's that Fay valued. These were to be packed up carefully, and Fay was to dig a hole in her backyard and bury them. This was a symbolic act of preserving the good things about George and the happy times they had spent together.

Fay carried out these tasks as directed. When she returned to the therapist, however, she reported that she had been unable to weep at the burial because "so much trash was not worth wasting tears over." She also reported that she was now feeling a lot better and was once again getting a good night's sleep. She no longer appeared depressed and seemed to be making good progress in the business of mourning and coming to terms with the loss of George.

Van der Hart (1983) discusses the use of rituals in psychotherapy, offering many examples. Van der Hart comments on the use, in many cultures, of such rituals as traditional rites of passage and healing rituals, and points out that western cultures have largely abandoned these activities. In many societies, puberty rites "mark the leap that children make to adolescence or adulthood," a process that is also accompanied by great changes in the family structure. These rites, however, exist only to a limited extent in our society; the Jewish Bar Mitzvah is one example of such a rite that has persisted. It may be because of this disappearance of ritual that young people develop their own "rites," whether these be wild parties, dancing to rock music, group delinquent activities, or coming together to get "high" on illicit drugs.

The problem Fay faced, in the case history recounted above, was also one of making a transition, and a fairly abrupt one at that. Carrying out the prescribed rituals, which were designed to have appropriate metaphorical meanings, seemed to help her make the needed transition.

Palazzoli et al. (1974) describe a similar "funeral rite," a ritual was prescribed for a family in which the two-and-a-half-year-old daughter, Marella, would not eat. This symptom appeared after the birth of Marella's baby brother, who suffered from an incurable congenital illness and had to remain in hospital. The parents decided not to tell Marella anything about the baby or his illness. When the baby died and the parents stopped visiting the hospital, Marella's anorexia became even worse.

The therapy team advised the parents to tell Marella the truth, and a ritual was devised as a means of doing this. The father was to tell Marella that her brother had died and was buried in the cemetery. Now it was important to bury his clothes also. The father dug a hole in the garden and the mother placed the baby's clothes in it, one by one. Marella then took a pair of little shoes and put them on top of the clothes. The parents were quite moved by this. The father then filled the hole with soil and planted a tree on top of it. After this Marella began to eat again and also started to talk about her brother, surprising her parents with her understanding of the situation.

Actions prescribed by the therapist to be performed during therapy sessions can also have metaphorical meanings. Papp (1982) describes the use of what she calls *couples choreography* in marital therapy, a technique whereby the marital relationship is defined metaphorically rather than literally. Papp points out that "explanatory language tends to isolate and fragment," whereas "figurative language tends to synthesize and combine." Couples choreography has much in common with *family sculpting* (Papp, 1980; Barker, 1981b, p. 122), which itself is an example of the use of metaphor in therapy. In this procedure family members are placed by the "sculptor," who is usually a family member, in positions and postures that represent aspects of their relationships and interactions with each other. The result is a tableau that can be observed and discussed. Various elements of family functioning can be sculpted—for example, closeness or power—and the present situation or the desired situation may be represented. A series of sculptures can also be created by different family members, showing how each of them perceives the family and how it functions.

Papp treats marital couples in groups of three or four couples. The marital partners are asked to close their eyes and have a "dream" or fantasy in which they visualize their spouses in whatever symbolic forms they would take in a dream. The result, Papp reports, is to create "a living, moving picture" that condenses complex relationships into "simple, eloquent images uncensored by logic." This is perhaps a poetic way of describing "right-brain" process; in any event, it has been found to facilitate therapy in certain cases.

Objects, too, may be used metaphorically. The cassette recorder referred to in the account of the Young family is an example. Angelo (1981) offers us another one: an envelope containing a blank sheet of paper was used in one instance to represent a family "secret"—an issue that family members were having difficulty confronting, the fact that the son in the family was adopted. By discussing what was "in the envelope," without specifying what it was, the family's resistance was overcome and the therapist was able to maintain control of the therapeutic process.

Later in the treatment of the same family a cloth puppet that had been used in previous sessions to represent the infantile aspects of the son was used in a similar way. The mother was told to repeat to the puppet statements considered by the therapist to be incongruent with other statements she had made. For example, she was asked to repeat her remark that she felt more at ease because over the past few days the son had been talking of getting married. In this case the metaphorical object, the puppet, was used to "discount some observed datum" and to pressure the mother to define herself in relation to the son, as a preferred alternative to offering her a verbal interpretation.

INDICATIONS FOR THE USE OF METAPHOR IN PSYCHOTHERAPY

It is important to assess the appropriateness of metaphor in psychotherapy. There are several criteria: the type of therapy being used, the clinical situation, the responsiveness of the client to more direct forms of communication, and the preferences and experience of the therapist.

Type of Therapy

Because talking or acting metaphorically are but ways of communicating, metaphor may in principle be used in any form of therapy in which therapists have to convey ideas or information to clients. It is more likely to be needed, however, the more complex the information to be imparted, the more "resistant" the client, and the more active the role of the therapist.

In psychoanalysis, in which the therapist's activities are confined largely to asking questions and making comments and interpretations, the usefulness of metaphor is probably limited. In behavior therapy the therapist is concerned, first, to discover the precise contingencies that are operating to maintain the symptoms and then, using operant or respondent methods, to devise a reinforcement or extinction schedule that will result in the disappearance of the symptoms and, often, their replacement by more functionally useful behaviors. Because crystal clear communication is necessary in this procedure, the usefulness of metaphor is likely to be limited. In both psychoanalysis and behavior therapy, metaphor may be useful in the initial stages when the nature of the proposed treatment is under discussion. It may also help, at critical points in such therapies, to motivate clients and sustain their interest.

Metaphor comes into its own, however, in those forms of treatment in which therapists play an active role in offering their clients ideas, instructions, solutions to consider, reframings, or other inputs which may or may not be immediately acceptable. These include most strategic and systemic therapies, hypnotherapy, and other relationship therapies; that is, those forms of treatment in which information (especially information that reframes situations) is exchanged between client and therapist in the context of a trusting relationship.

The Clinical Situation

Because it is an indirect method of communication, metaphor is of particular value in those clinical situations in which direct communication is ineffective. In discussing Milton Erickson's use of anecdotes, Zeig (1980) has pointed out that the more his patients resisted his ideas the more indirect and anecdotal Erickson became.

Let us consider a few clinical situations in which communication by metaphor may be useful. First, metaphor may help to motivate dispirited or pessimistic clients who are doubtful whether their problems are soluble. One might use anecdotes, for example, about dispirited people (or animals, Muppets, or the like) who were able to find a way of becoming motivated again.

Second, metaphor may be useful when treatment is impeded by the unwillingness of clients to accept ideas the therapist is trying to communicate to them.

Third, indirect communication through metaphor may be helpful when the direct expression of ideas would upset clients and, very likely, damage the relationship between therapist and client. An example of such a situation is to be found in the case vignette at the start of this chapter.

Fourth, metaphor may enliven the interest of clients who are getting bored or restless and whose concentration is lapsing. Children seen in family therapy, for example, often have a hard time attending to the direct discussion of issues. Stories, games and activities, all of which can be devised with metaphorical meaning, generally suit them better.

Finally, in the "utilization" phase of hypnotherapy—that is the phase after trance has been induced—metaphor may be very useful. Erickson made extensive use of anecdotes during hypnotherapy, as well as during therapy without trance. Many therapists agree with Lankton and Lankton (1983) that the use of multiple metaphors in the course of hypnotherapy enables subjects to make especially effective use of the resources available to them in their unconscious. The presentation of a succession of metaphors, and the ambiguity of the metaphors themselves, offer a lot of choice at the unconscious level.

The use of metaphors in the course of hypnotherapy will not be emphasized in this book. Readers wishing further information on the subject should consult *The Answer Within* (Lankton and Lankton, 1983) and the collected papers of Erickson himself (Erickson, 1980a,b,c,d,). It is worth pointing out, however, that most of the therapeutic procedures that can be carried out in trance can also be carried out in the alert state; the reverse is also true.

The Responsiveness of Clients to Direct Communication

In the assessment phase before therapy is started it is good practice to take careful note of clients' communication styles. With some, direct communication comes naturally, and therapy can often be successfully accomplished with little use of indirect methods. Others appear to accept direct communications easily but intellectualize to such an extent that change is not readily brought about. With these individuals, as with those who naturally communicate indirectly, it may be wise to communicate ideas metaphorically. Those who tend naturally to communicate indirectly may be recognized by their frequent use of similes, metaphors, and analogies, by their telling of stories to illustrate points, and sometimes by a poetic way of speaking. They often appear less concerned about the factual information they are conveying than about the effect they are having on those to whom they are speaking.

Although Milton Erickson was highly skilled in using metaphors both therapeutically and in teaching, quite frequently he also used direct methods. Largely on the basis of interviews with therapists who worked closely with Erickson, Hammond (1984) maintains that at the height of his powers Erickson used direct methods some 80 percent of the time. This observation helps put metaphor and other indirect methods into proper perspective: in most cases, these techniques should probably play an adjunct role.

Therapists' Preferences and Experience

Stories and other forms of metaphorical communication come more easily to some people than to others. A degree of confidence and a feeling of ease when telling stories are prerequisites for the use of this approach in therapy. Therapists can develop these qualities by first practicing storytelling in settings other than therapy sessions. Then they can start telling short anecdotes during sessions, starting with issues of minor significance—perhaps quite peripheral to the main issues being addressed in the therapy —only gradually coming to use stories as a major therapeutic device. When therapists are confident and practiced in using anecdotes and short stories during therapy, they may wish to develop skills in other metaphorical methods, such as are discussed in the remainder of this book.

METAPHORS FOR THE TREATMENT PROCESS

Metaphors can be helpful when proposed treatment plans are being discussed with clients or their families. They can assist in explaining the nature of a particular problem and how the therapy plan may help resolve it. Most psychiatric problems have multiple causes, and in discussing the respective roles of biological, intrapsychic, and social factors, metaphors from the animal and plant kingdoms may be used. Plants may fail to grow properly because there is something constitutionally wrong with them; for example, they may be the wrong variety for the prevailing soil or for the conditions at the time the seeds are sown or the seedlings transplanted. They may be subject to some disease process, perhaps inborn or perhaps acquired; or the growing conditions may be unsuitable and need to be modified.

Metaphors for family problems can similarly be found in the plant kingdom. A family situation may resemble, metaphorically, a jungle or a garden growing wild or overgrown with weeds; plants may have insufficient space in which to grow and develop, or their growth may be constrained as a result of too much watering or pruning, or from being battered by storms. The growth and development of children may be adversely affected in analogous ways.

SUMMARY

Among the uses of metaphors in psychotherapy are the following: making points, suggesting solutions to problems, decreasing resistance and increasing motivation, reframing situations, helping people recognize themselves and their resources, and controlling the therapeutic relationship. In addition, story telling is a common way of communicating in metaphor. Actions, relationships, questions, and objects can all have metaphorical potential in psychotherapy.

Although metaphor probably has a place in most types of therapy, its greatest usefulness may be in those therapies in which the therapist plays an active part in helping the clients make specific, defined changes. These include many forms of strategic and systemic therapies, as well as hypnotherapy. Metaphor can be valuable when direct forms of communication prove ineffective; it avoids direct confrontation, which some clients find difficult to deal with, and it is a way of communicating ideas that may be unacceptable to clients at the conscious level.

Stories and other metaphorical devices can enliven therapy when those taking part are getting bored or an impasse has been reached. The skills needed to use metaphor can be learned and are a useful addition to the therapist's psychotherapeutic tools.

A PRACTICAL EXERCISE

A couple you are seeing ask for help with some marital problems. They are having difficulty, however, in accepting the idea that they should be seen together rather than separately. Devise a metaphorical approach to helping them understand that treatment is likely to be more effective if they attend together.

3

The Various Types
of Metaphor

Howard and his friend, Ian, both bought new word processing programs for their computers. They were impressed by the power of the new programs and the number of things the salesperson assured them they could do.

The instructions came in a large volume of many pages. Anxious to use his new toy, Howard skimmed through the instructions, looking for the bare essentials that he needed to get started. He soon found that he could quickly do things that were out of the question with his old program. It was easy to move big blocks of text around, to correct misspellings, and to change names and descriptions throughout a whole file with hardly more than the touch of a key. Compared with the rather primitive—if less expensive—program he had used before, it was like driving a Rolls Royce after a Volkswagen Beetle.

There were some minor disappointments. Howard found that reforming paragraphs wasn't quite as easy as he had expected, though it was easier than it had been with his old program. Underlining seemed to require hitting two keys in succession, and subscripts and superscripts were also a little difficult to achieve. So the program's performance did not quite live up to Howard's expectations.

But Howard was a busy writer. He was always working hard to meet deadlines and he was pleased to find he could progress faster with his new aid than he had been able to do before. Such was the pressure of his work schedule that he kept on delaying a detailed study of the program's instructions.

Ian, who bought the same program, approached things rather differently. He started by studying the manual carefully. It took him several evenings to absorb all the information in it, but he didn't start to use the program until he had completed his study. He too was pleased with the new program, and his productivity improved greatly. He did not have any of Howard's reservations about the program's performance.

Ian had been using the program for several months when he and Howard had occasion to work on an article together. As they collaborated, making changes to the text, adding sections, deleting others, and moving blocks of text around, Ian realized that Howard was unaware of many of the program's features. He did not do several things he could have done, and some of the things he was doing could have been done more simply. After some hesitation—he didn't want to upset his friend—Ian mentioned some features of the program of which Howard seemed unaware. Howard listened, surprised and a bit embarrassed that he had been using the program for several months without understanding many of its possibilities. The time Ian had spent studying the manual systematically had obviously been well spent.

Despite his heavy work schedule, Howard at last put aside a couple of evenings to study the manual. As he did so, he was amazed at how much more there was to the program than he had realized. And when he put his newly acquired knowledge to use, the burden of composing and editing text became lighter than he had ever thought possible.

A CLASSIFICATION OF THERAPEUTIC METAPHORS

We will consider metaphors used in psychotherapy under seven general headings:

1. Major stories designed to deal comprehensively with complex clinical situations.
2. Anecdotes and short stories aimed at achieving specific, limited goals.
3. Analogies, similes and brief metaphorical statements or phrases that illustrate or emphasize specific points
4. Relationship metaphors.
5. Tasks with metaphorical meanings. These may be carried out during therapy sessions, like the "couples choreography" of Papp (1982), mentioned in the previous chapter; or they may be prescribed to be done between sessions, like the task given Fay (as described in Chapter 2).
6. Metaphorical objects. These are objects used during therapy to represent something other than they actually are.
7. Artistic metaphors. These are drawings, paintings, clay models or other artistic productions which symbolize other things. Artistic Metaphors were developed and created by Crowley and Mills (1984) and can be found in detail in their book entitled *Therapeutic Metaphors for Children and the Child Within* (1986, in press).

Although this classification is not exhaustive, it covers the great majority of metaphorical devices available for use in psychotherapy and includes all those discussed in this book. There is some overlap among categories; nevertheless, it is important to know what general types of therapeutic metaphor are available for use and which types are likely to be effective in particular clinical situations. Like Howard in our opening vignette, therapists will be able to get maximum value out of this technique once they have studied it carefully.

Major Metaphorical Stories

Major metaphorical stories are carefully planned and developed to achieve major therapeutic goals. The fullest account of how to construct them is found in Gordon's (1978) book *Therapeutic Metaphors*. The use of such stories is not indicated unless the therapist has a good understanding of the case; only a thorough assessment will yield sufficient information to construct a

detailed metaphor and one that is isomorphic with the actual
clinical situation. One must also have clear therapeutic goals; the
establishment of desired treatment outcomes is discussed fully
in the next chapter.

Gordon (1978) is much influenced both by the work of Virginia
Satir and by the models of communication and therapy put forward by the developers of *neurolinguistic programming*, or NLP
(Bandler & Grinder, 1979; Dilts et al., 1980). Thus he advocates
paying special attention to the *style* of communication of each of
the subjects whose problem the metaphor addresses. He adopts
Satir's (1972) classification of communication styles, categoriz-
ing people as "placaters," "blamers," "computers," "distract-
ers," and "levelers," advocating taking these into account in the
development of therapeutic metaphors.

Gordon also stresses the importance of the "representational
systems" used by the subjects, a key concept of neurolinguistic
programming. For most people, either the visual, the auditory,
or the kinesthetic system serves as a primary channel for processing information. By taking into account the representational
systems used by clients, and wording stories accordingly, Gordon maintains, therapists may make metaphors even more isomorphic and thus more effective. Taking these points into account is important also in developing rapport with clients (see
Chapter 11).

Once the assessment of the family, marital couple, or other
group or individual is complete, the next step is to construct, or
invent, characters that are equivalent to, or *isomorphic* with, the
real-life people concerned. Consider the Jones family, composed
of a father, a mother, a son, a daughter, and an adopted daughter, who sought help because of the children's violent fights. We
might invent an imaginary family that includes two parents, a
daughter, a son, and a foster son, as suggested in Table 1.

Next the significant events of the case must be represented by
equivalent events or incidents in the story. This of course is possible only when a full assessment of the case has been completed;
otherwise, the therapist will not know which are the significant
events. Table 2 presents a possible scenario.

Table 1
A Real-Life Family and Their Metaphoric Counterparts

Real Life	Metaphor
Father (Harold)	Father (Ivan) in newly-opened foster home
Mother (Jane)	Mother (Karen)
Son (Lance), age 17	Daughter (Mary), age 16
Daughter (Nancy), age 12	Son (Oscar), age 13
Adopted daughter (Pamela), age 6	Foster-son (Quentin), age 5

We have now constructed an imaginary foster home containing characters who, we believe, are isomorphic with the family we are treating. We have also distinguished a number of behaviors and relationships that we believe are important in the life and problems of the family, and we have tried to reproduce these behaviors and relationships, isomorphically, in the metaphor we are constructing.

Table 2
A Metaphoric Scenario

Real Life	Metaphor
Mother favors her son, Lance	Ivan always takes his daughter, Mary's, side in disputes
Lance orders his sisters about a lot	Mary is put in charge of the younger children
Nancy resents Pamela and fights with her	Oscar loses his temper with Quentin
Harold and Jane disagree over what to do about the children's fights	Ivan and Karen are at loggerheads about how to deal with the situation

The next step is to plan how to use the metaphor to help the family achieve their desired outcomes. The outcomes they are seeking will have been determined during the diagnostic assessment. What Gordon (1978) calls a *connecting strategy* is now required, as suggested by Figure 1.

According to Gordon, it is not usually sufficient to present a ready-made solution in the metaphor; one cannot successfully jump straight from "the problem" to "the new behavior." Instead the metaphor has to show *how* the characters representing the real-life subjects (the clients being treated) made the changes that enabled them to overcome their problems. This is the connecting strategy; it might be that they had a long discussion and considered the pros and cons of various courses of action, or that they came to see the situation in an entirely different light (in other words it became reframed). It is possible to offer several connecting strategies: The issues may be discussed; they may be seen to be less important than the parties concerned formerly thought; courses of action they had never previously considered may occur to them; and the motives of each of them might be redefined. Indeed, this is often what clients have been trying to do on their own, unsuccessfully. What is usually needed is some kind of "reframing" of the problem behaviors, feelings, or situation. This will then be the connecting strategy.

How could we reframe the problem behaviors we have been presented with by the family we are considering? Let us consider each of the four features, identified in Table 2, of the relationship structure in this family. To take the last-listed feature first,

Problem	*Connecting Strategy*	*Desired Outcome*
Nancy fights with Pamela	?	Nancy and Pamela learn to get along with each other
The parents disagree about how to deal with the situation	?	The parents see eye-to-eye on how to deal with the children

Figure 1. Getting from problem to desired outcome.

we know that Harold and Jane disagree over what to do about the fights between Nancy and Pamela. At times their disagreements become quite heated. This situation could be reframed as showing that they are both deeply concerned about the children; it is clearly important to them to be good parents, doing their best for their children.

Nancy's resentment of Pamela, the adopted daughter, appears to have arisen as a reaction to the special concern shown by the parents for Pamela. The family adopted Pamela when she was 4 years old. Before this, Pamela had been in a succession of foster homes after she was separated from her abusive, natural family. Harold and Jane felt they must take special care of this little girl and give her extra attention, so as to make her feel wanted and secure.

The second feature shown in Table 2 can be reframed as reflecting the fact that although Lance was somewhat bossy toward his younger sisters, he was nevertheless showing his interest in and concern for them. Jane's tendency to favor Lance over her daughters can be reframed as commendable pride in her son and his considerable academic achievements. Her pride was fully justified, but she had not perhaps considered that it might cause some resentment on the part of the other two children.

The above points could have been made directly to the family, and with some families that would be a good way to proceed. The Jones family, though, had proved themselves resistant to direct input of this sort, and a metaphorical approach therefore seemed more likely to succeed. The points the therapist wanted to make were therefore incorporated into the following story about the foster family.

> I've been thinking about a family I saw when I was working in Toronto. It was quite an interesting situation. Ivan was 39 and worked as an insurance appraiser and Karen, who was 37, worked part-time as a cashier at a gas station. Ivan and Karen had two children of their own: Mary, aged 16, was a successful high school student, and Oscar, aged 13, was also doing well at school.

Once their children had both become teenagers, Ivan and Karen decided they would like to open up their home to a foster child. So they applied to the Children's Aid Society to become foster parents. They had several interviews with C.A.S. staff and were visited in their home by their foster care worker. Ivan and Karen were pleased when at last they were told they were approved as foster parents; their social worker said she believed they had excellent potential in this work. They weren't surprised because they had always been a happy family who had got along well together and enjoyed each other's company.

Quentin, an attractive-looking five-year-old, was their first foster child. He came from a difficult background. During his first two years of life he had been badly abused and neglected. He had then been taken into care, but had subsequently had a very unsettled time before coming to Ivan and Karen. The social worker had warned them that he might be difficult; in previous foster homes he had been quite aggressive, which had caused him to be moved several times. But Ivan and Karen felt strongly committed to being good foster parents and felt they had a lot to offer a boy like Quentin. Before Quentin's arrival, while they were having some preparatory visits with him, they spent a lot of time thinking about what they should do to provide the best environment for him. They wanted to make him feel at home and secure—perhaps for the first time in his life—and they even hoped they might at some time in the future be able to adopt him.

It wasn't long before Quentin started to test out his new family. He became defiant and started to react with tantrums when limits were placed on his behavior. Ivan and Karen found themselves spending a lot of time dealing with these problems; some days Quentin virtually monopolized their attention. They managed to hold Quentin to the limits they had decided on and to handle his tantrums quite well, though at times they had to restrain him physically.

After a few months Quentin seemed at last to be settling into his new home, and his foster parents began to feel that the worst was over. But then Oscar, the 13-year-old, began to present behavioral problems. Particularly trying were the arguments he and Quentin got into. These became steadily worse until the two boys seemed to be almost constantly fighting.

Sometimes Mary was left to babysit the boys—usually when both parents were working. She did her best to act as mediator between Oscar and Quentin but unfortunately she began herself to get involved in their disputes. I'm sure she was trying to help, but the way things worked out she was constantly shouting at the boys and lecturing them; this didn't seem to help matters and further disturbed what had previously been a peaceful and happy household.

Now Ivan and Mary, the family's first child, had always been close. Ivan was very proud of Mary and her excellent performance at school and in sports. They were both good skiers and often went skiing together, something Karen didn't much enjoy. I guess it wasn't too surprising that when Mary started getting into disputes with Oscar and Quentin, Ivan usually took her side; moreover, being an intelligent child, she usually had a good argument to put forward to justify her point of view and actions.

Ivan and Karen didn't know what to do about the continual arguing and fighting in the family; what had been a happy family was fast turning into a nightmare. They spent long hours discussing what they should do, but found it hard to agree on a plan of action. In fact quite the opposite happened, and they, too, found themselves increasingly in disagreement; they sometimes got into quite violent arguments themselves, which was a new development.

The more Ivan and Karen tried to decide on a common course of action the deeper their divisions became; and all the while Oscar and Quentin fought even more fiercely and more often. The parents began to worry that Oscar, who was becoming increasingly bad-tempered, might hurt Quentin.

Unsure what was happening and what they should do, the troubled parents managed to agree that they should seek the advice of their family doctor. He referred them to a counselor in the hope that family therapy might help.

One day about this time Ivan and Karen had a particularly heated row. Ivan noticed that afterwards the children's behavior seemed to be even worse than usual. He pointed this out to Karen.

"Do you think" he said to her, "that it could be our own arguments and shouting matches that make the children fight?"

"Of course not," Karen replied, dismissing the point. "They started fighting long before we did."

Ivan wasn't so sure he was on the wrong track, so he raised the matter with their therapist. The therapist didn't feel able to give them a firm opinion right away. He did make certain observations, though. He was very impressed, he told them, with the amount of caring the parents showed for Quentin. He told them that in his experience few foster parents gave as much devoted attention to a new child in their home as they had. He was impressed, too, by the care Mary had been showing to both the boys, and by how hard she had been trying to help them settle their differences. Oscar, he thought, was probably jealous of the new boy in the house, especially one who needed so much attention. Perhaps in their efforts to do everything they could for Quentin, they had temporarily overlooked Oscar's needs.

The parents asked the therapist which of their methods of dealing with the children was best, or were both of them on the wrong track? He suggested they try an experiment. For one week they should use Ivan's methods and for the next they should use Karen's. They spun a coin to see whose methods would be used first; Karen won. The therapist's only stipulation was that for each week both parents would use identical methods, even if each disagreed with what the other one advocated. He made just one other suggestion: they should both observe Oscar carefully to see if they thought he was jealous of his foster brother.

The results of the experiment were surprising. The children behaved much better during both weeks, and the parents found it impossible to decide which of the weeks was the better. This was remarkable because Ivan's and Karen's methods were quite different, Ivan's being a lot stricter. Precisely how the children were handled didn't seem to matter as much as having Ivan and Karen work together did. Despite observing Oscar closely, as their therapist had requested, Ivan and Karen didn't detect much evidence of jealousy on his part; in fact he seemed to thrive on being observed.

In cold print therapeutic metaphors are less lifelike and convincing than they are in the context of a warm, mutually respectful treatment relationship. The nonverbal component of the telling is important too, of course, including the emphasis put on different words and phrases. Metaphors such as the one above are also likely to be more effective if they are part of a series of stories told in the course of therapy.

Although the unexpected can be powerful, major metaphors are usually better received if they are not the first story told to a client or family. Once people have got used to having their therapist tell them tales they usually accept them with little question. The therapist's objective should be to have the story received without much conscious consideration of why it is being recounted; metaphor is effective, it seems, because it is a means of establishing communication with the "right brain." Precisely because logical arguments, and rational considerations, have not led to adaptive behavior, attitudinal change—which, according to Watzlawick (1978) whose views now seem to have wide acceptance, is apparently the business mainly of the right cerebral hemisphere and is largely an unconscious process—is required. This issue is addressed further in Chapter 11. The timing of metaphors, especially longer and more complex ones, is thus very important—perhaps as important as their content.

Some other points about this story are worth noting. The sexes of the children were reversed and their ages were altered slightly to help make the story different from the real-life situation while yet remaining isomorphic with it. This story did remain quite similar to the real-life situation it was designed to represent, a fact that may be criticized. When stories are too much like real-life situations, clients may perceive the similarities consciously and begin to object to the arguments and points of view put forward metaphorically. The main reason for using metaphor is to present the points "in disguise," so that, unlike direct therapy methods, they are not questioned at the conscious level. In other words, the aim is to present a meaning metaphorically to the right brain, not in logical, digital language to the left brain.

"Digital" communication was defined by Watzlawick and his colleagues (1967), who liken it to the functioning of digital computers. These convert both data and instructions into numbers, so that there is only an arbitrary correspondence between the information and its digital expression. "Digital" language similarly uses arbitrary symbols (with the very occasional exception of onomatopoeic words), for example, "d–o–g" for a type of animal or "c–h–a–i–r" for a particular article of furniture; but the meanings of these symbols, though arbitrary, are usually quite precise and indeed are defined in dictionaries.

Unlike digital computers, analogic computers and machines deal with "discrete positive magnitudes—the analogues of the data (p. 60). . . . In analogic communication there *is* something 'thing-like' in what is used to express the thing. Analogic communication can more readily be referred to the thing it stands for" (Watzlawick et al., 1967, p. 62). Metaphors are analogic in that, if properly constructed and delivered, they evoke ideas, feelings and attitudes, and direct attention to the relationships between people and things, without offering specific, digital input, such as would be subject to rational, logical scrutiny.

In practice, the therapist must make a clinical judgment as to how similar a metaphor should be to a client's actual situation. The crucial issue is what the metaphor conveys at the unconscious level and the extent to which it enables a client to obtain a new view of a situation—to reframe it.

Anecdotes and Short Stories

Short stories and anecdotes can readily be used in most stages of therapy to make specific points or to achieve other, limited therapeutic aims. An anecdote does not require such careful preparation as a full-length metaphorical story; one usually need not trouble to make everything isomorphic with the real-life situation. The anecdote simply illustrates or emphasizes a particular point.

All of us have had experiences that we can describe in order to make points in metaphorical form. Milton Erickson's tales, however, provide a particularly rich source of anecdotes suitable for use in therapy. A tale I have found useful is Erickson's (1980e) story of Joe:

> When Joe was a boy his behavior was incorrigibly bad. He could not be contained in his school or his community, and at the age of 12 he was sent to the Boys' Industrial School, a permanent home for delinquent children who could not be handled in an ordinary home for delinquents. After three years at the school Joe was given leave to visit his parents, but on the way home he committed some felonies. As a result, he was arrested and returned to the school.
>
> At the age of 21 Joe had to be discharged by law. He went to Milwaukee and almost immediately committed armed robbery and burglary. This led to the first of a series of prison terms; as soon as Joe would get out of prison, he would commit further offenses and find himself back inside again. In prison he was an exceptionally difficult prisoner and spent much of his time in solitary confinement.
>
> When Joe was released at the end of one of his prison terms, he returned to the village in Wisconsin where his family lived. A few days later all three stores in the village were robbed and a powerboat was found missing from its moorings.
>
> A day or two later Joe met the talented and beautiful daughter of a rich local farmer; he asked her if he could take her to the village dance on Friday night.
>
> "You can, if you are a gentleman," Edye replied.
>
> Joe and Edye went to the dance and danced together all evening. The next morning all three merchants whose goods had been stolen found their merchandise returned, and the powerboat reappeared at its moorings.
>
> Joe then asked Edye's father for a job on the farm. He was hired and proved an excellent worker. In due course Joe married Edye, inherited the farm, became chairman of the local school board, and helped in the rehabilitation of prisoners released from the local jail. And all the therapy he ever experienced was, "You can, if you are a gentleman" (summarized from Erickson, 1980e, pp. 211–216).

This anecdote, which for best therapeutic effect should be re-counted in fuller form and after the therapist has studied Erick-son's original account of it, offers its hearers a number of mes-sages. Among these are the following:

- Discontinuous change is possible.
- Big changes can occur without intensive, or indeed any, psychotherapy.
- There comes a time in people's lives when they are ready to make changes.
- A healthy relationship, perhaps especially with a member of the opposite sex, can work wonders.

The story of Joe is a useful one to tell those who do not believe that people, such as the hardened delinquent, can change at all, let alone quickly. It can help motivate families who are on the point of giving up on treatment, and it may help reframe "hope-less" situations as offering some hope after all.

Analogies, Similes, and Other Brief Metaphorical Statements

Analogies and similes are commonly used as a part of the English language. We refer to the "point" of a joke as well as to the "point" of a needle, and we speak of "riding high" when we do not refer to the process of riding a horse or anything else. Such metaphorical phrases can be used effectively in the course of psychotherapy, just as they can in other forms of conversa-tion. They sometimes offer useful alternatives to the direct state-ment of ideas, especially ideas that the person being addressed may be reluctant to accept when they are presented directly.

Sports activities provide many opportunities for the use of metaphorical phrases. In North America the baseball-derived phrase "getting to first base" is a good example. Thus a therapist might describe a person's problem as being that of "getting to first base," rather than as "getting started" with something, or achieving the first part of a task. To someone with an interest in baseball this might be a meaningful and more acceptable phrase. To a baseball coach it might readily facilitate a recommendation that the person concerned practice whatever the task might be that is presenting difficulty.

In cricket there is a useful phrase, "sticky wicket." A sticky wicket is said to exist when the playing field is drying in the sun after rain; batting in such conditions is difficult because such a field is particularly conducive to spin, which can make the ball bounce in ways that are hard for the batsman to anticipate. The bowler therefore has an advantage and the batsman's skills are sorely taxed. Thus to a person who understands and enjoys cricket, a phrase like, "It sounds as if you were on a pretty sticky wicket," may be more meaningful and acceptable than saying, "It seems you were in a difficult situation." If the person is a skilled cricketer who can deal well with a sticky wicket, the use of such a phrase may suggest, unconsciously if not consciously, that he or she can cope with the situation that is actually under discussion.

Metaphors are available from many areas of life other than sports; in fact almost any activity may be used as the subject of a metaphorical allusion. Resources not being actively used may be compared to money in the bank. Some of the decisions parents and children have to make as children grow up can be likened to deciding when to remove the training wheels from a bicycle. The metaphor of a ship going through stormy seas may be used with people whose lives are in turmoil. The fact that storms at sea are always succeeded by calm may provide helpful reassurance.

Relationship Metaphors

A relationship metaphor uses one relationship as a metaphor for another, as in the vignette at the start of Chapter 2. The therapist in that session wished to raise a question about the relationship between the family members who were present at the interview, and the father, who was not. The therapist wondered if the father's absence was in some way due to the rather distant relationship which, the therapist suspected, existed between the father and the other family members. Perhaps the other family members had discouraged the father from attending, even though this may not have been their conscious intent. To have raised this issue directly might have caused the family members present to adopt a defensive posture; they might have felt they were being criticized or attacked, which would probably have been anti-therapeutic. By raising the issue metaphorically and suggesting that perhaps he himself had done something to upset the father, the therapist expected to be able to avoid this trap, as indeed he did.

Relationships of many kinds can be used therapeutically. In a family in which the two children were quite out of the control of their single mother, the relationship between the oldest child and his dog was used as a metaphor for that between mother and children. The dog was as much out of his master's control as his master was out of his mother's, and the mother was able to learn much about controlling children from the discussion the therapist had with the son about controlling his dog.

Family therapy presents many opportunities to use relationship metaphors, both diagnostically and therapeutically. The therapist's relationship with one family member, perhaps a child, can be a metaphor for the relationship between another member, perhaps a parent, and the child. A therapeutic device that which can sometimes be powerful is to model desired behavior during therapy sessions. Thus, rather than tell a father how to talk effectively to his son, the therapist can talk to the boy in the appropriate way. By this means the father can be shown a different way of communicating with his son and can be helped to develop the kind of relationship he would like to have with him. The relationship between the therapist and the boy thus becomes a metaphor for the relationship between father and son.

Relationships between families, or particular family members, and people or agencies outside the family (school staff, social agencies, landlords, and the like) can be dealt with in a similar way. An example is afforded by a family, one of whose children was in the care of a statutory child welfare agency. The relationship between this family and their social worker was a poor one;

the parents hated the social worker and could find nothing good to say about her. They desperately wanted their daughter back but felt so angry with the social worker that they were never able to have a rational discussion with her on the subject of the girl's return home. A session was arranged at which the parents and the social worker were present. The therapist used this to model a different relationship with the social worker. After spending some time establishing rapport with the social worker the therapist engaged her in conversation on several of the issues about which the parents were concerned. Gradually he handed the conversation over to the parents to continue and they were able to have a more constructive discussion of the points at issue than they had ever done previously. This process is often referred to as "modeling," but it is also an example of using one relationship as a metaphor for another.

Tasks With Metaphorical Meanings

The use of rituals has already been referred to and an example (the case of Fay and George) was described in Chapter 2. Most tasks with metaphorical meanings that are prescribed as part of psychotherapy have a ritualistic element to them; it is not necessary, for our purposes, to make a sharp distinction between tasks and rituals. Not all tasks that are given during therapy have metaphorical meanings. Thus if a couple are asked to go home and spend a certain amount of time discussing what they want to achieve from marital therapy, their task probably does not involve the use of metaphor, unless the idea of marital therapy is being used as a metaphor for something else, such as a business partnership.

Onno van der Hart (1983), in his book *Rituals in Psychotherapy*, lists a number of uses of rituals, emphasizing their value in helping people and families negotiate developmental stages. Some uses of rituals mentioned by van der Hart are described in the next paragraphs.

Removing discrepancies. By a *discrepancy*, van der Hart means the use in one context of a behavior that is appropriate and even useful in another situation, but not in the one in which it is being used. For example, when a colleague of van der Hart's came home for supper every night he was still occupied, in thought, with his work. The family found this difficult, and the subject himself wanted to give more attention to his family. A private ritual in which he washed and changed his clothes before dinner helped overcome this problem.

Establishing order and stability. Suggesting or prescribing rituals for a family to carry out itself conveys a message: order can replace chaos. "The myth upon which the ritual is based describes a world in which chaos is being, or is to be, replaced by order" (Wallace, quoted in van der Hart, 1983).

Relabeling or reframing. A ritual can provide a framework in which a symptom can be seen to have value. Thus a young woman's anorexia was relabeled "fasting" and described as a behavior that belongs to the stage of transition from childhood to womanhood. Fasting was prescribed, in the company of two companions, until the subject was able to indicate that she had made the transition and could join in regular meals.

Permitting the symbolic expression of feelings. Burial rituals and other rites of mourning are examples of the symbolic expression of feelings. Celebrations marking the accomplishment of therapeutic and other tasks serve a similar function.

Transforming family structure. The very act of performing a ritual can produce change in a family, because it induces family members to behave in ways in which they have not, presumably, behaved before. This itself may have a symbolic significance; indeed, it should have if the ritual has been well designed to meet the family's needs.

Coppersmith (1983) describes the "burial" of the medication of a girl who had been labeled "hyperactive." In the course of therapy with this child's family, it had become apparent that the process of labeling the girl "abnormal," or hyperactive, had had adverse effects on the family system. The burial of the medicine was part of the process of relabeling the girl "normal." Not only a burial ritual but a relabeling ritual, this device probably also served to promote order and stability in the family.

Coppersmith (1985) also describes a ritual in which marriage partners who had been unable to talk openly about an important past event were asked to describe on paper, each separately, the event that was affecting them so profoundly in the present. Without looking at them, the therapist put the pieces of paper in a small box, and then asked the couple to bury the box in the ground outside. It was January and the ground was hard. The "frozen ground" served, Coppersmith points out, as a metaphor for the couple's "frozen relationship." The ritual seems to have had a markedly beneficial effect.

Metaphorical Objects

Angelo's (1981) paper, describing the metaphorical use of such objects as an envelope with a blank piece of paper in it and a cloth puppet, has already been referred to (Chapter 2). Although the published literature specifically addressing the metaphorical use of objects is limited, objects are used in this way quite extensively.

Metaphorical objects are used as a major feature of play therapy with children. Sometimes children will express, and work through, their feelings about family members and other people in their world, by playing in a dollhouse with dolls representing family figures—a metaphorical use of these figures. Sometimes there is more "metaphorical disguise"; toy animals may be used, but so also may inanimate toys, such as cars, trucks, railroad rolling stock, and ships. Other things that may be used as metaphorical objects include ambulances, fire trucks and guns, tanks, fighter planes and other weapons of war. These all tend to have special symbolic significance.

Artistic Metaphors

Crowley and Mills's original work (1984, 1986) with Artistic Metaphors allows children to draw upon their own inner resources of unconscious learnings and abilities to resolve emotional as well as physiological problems. These metaphors are artistic productions, such as drawings, paintings, clay or plasticine models, structures built with "Lego" or any other production representing a feeling state, experience, or something else that may be of significance in the treatment process.

In their work Crowley and Mills say, for example, that if children are angry or in pain, they may be asked to draw "angry"— to show the therapist what "it" looks like. ("It" need not be defined; the right brain is not particular about such logical niceties). Or they may be asked to draw their pain, and then to draw what "it" looks like when the pain is better. The next step might be to draw what would help to get "it" better.

Crowley and Mills suggest Artistic Metaphors are useful when one wants to reframe a subject's experience in another sensory modality. Thus a child who describes an experience in auditory or kinesthetic terms might be asked to draw it, thus converting it to the visual modality and becoming able to view it from a new perspective. This is a useful device child therapists may use to establish effective communication with their clients.

SUMMARY

There are many metaphorical ways of communicating. All have the potential to be of use in the course of psychotherapy. It is important for the therapist to know about the different types of metaphor, the clinical situations in which each may be useful, and how to use each type.

The principal types of metaphor that may be of use during psychotherapy are: Elaborate stories designed to deal comprehensively with particular clinical situations; anecdotes and shorter stories designed to achieve limited therapeutic goals in the course of therapy; analogies, similes, and brief metaphorical statements or phrases used to illustrate or emphasize specific points; relationship metaphors, in which the therapist/client or another relationship is used to suggest something about some other relationship; rituals and tasks with metaphorical meanings; and artistic metaphors—artistic productions representing things of clinical significance. Artistic metaphors can lead to more effective communication with children. In addition, objects themselves may be used metaphorically, not only in play therapy with children, but also in therapy with adults and families.

Metaphorical communication should be used only when the therapist understands properly how to use it. It is important also to have a clear therapeutic plan and an understanding of how any metaphors fit into such a plan. As an illustration, a new word-processing program may offer many possibilities, but best results are likely when the operator is familiar with all the features of the program and understands properly how each may be used most effectively.

A PRACTICAL EXERCISE

You are seeing a family of four members. There are behavioral problems with both the children, Robert, aged 17 and Clifton, aged 10. When the family arrive for the third family session, Robert is absent. The parents say that he refused to come and they cannot see any way they can make him; he is a big boy, stronger than they are, and there is no way they can force him to attend.

Devise an anecdote, a task with metaphorical meaning, and a relationship metaphor, each of which might assist the family in getting Robert to attend future sessions.

4

Establishing
Treatment Goals

Two tanker truck drivers named Jack and Jill worked for different employers. One summer there was a severe water shortage in their town, and both employers decided to use their trucks to bring water into the town.

Jack's employer was well organized, systematic, and efficient. Before dispatching Jack to fetch a load of water he made inquiries as to where a supply of clean water, suitable for drinking, could be obtained. Then he had Jack study the map to discover the quickest route to the place where he was to fill up with water.

Jill's employer was more casual. He knew that there were a number of places in the surrounding area where water was available, so he told Jill to drive in the general direction of the nearest large town until she found someone who would let her fill up her tanker at a reasonable price. Jill did as she was told, but things didn't turn out to be as easy as she had been led to expect. Several times she ended up in what she thought were likely places, only to have to turn round and retrace her route when she found either that water was unavailable, or available only at an exorbitant price. Eventually, though, she found a water supply, filled her tank and returned to her home town.

Meanwhile Jack had driven straight to the supplier of water selected by his employer. He filled his tank up right away, and obtained a certificate, provided by the local health department, indicating that the water in his tank was fit to drink. He arrived back at his base in half the time it took Jill to get back. Jack's employer had no difficulty selling the water to the thirsty townsfolk, helped greatly by the certificate that reassured them that it was safe to drink. The transaction was quite profitable for him.

Jill arrived back long after Jack. By this time most of the urgent demand for water in the town had been satisfied. The water Jill had brought was also more expensive than Jack's and there was doubt about its purity. It sold only slowly, and Jill's employer was therefore unable to send for another load that day, though Jack fetched and sold, on his employer's behalf, two loads by sundown.

OUTCOME FRAMING

Most human endeavors go better with planning, preparation, and the setting of well-defined objectives. Psychotherapy is no exception, though some schools of therapy place more emphasis on the setting of objectives than others do. Haley (1976) makes the point that a successful outcome is possible only if therapy starts with clearly defined goals. Otherwise there is no way of knowing whether you have achieved success. Moreover the goals must be defined in such a way that therapist and client can each see clearly whether they have been met.

The term *outcome frame* has been extensively used by the developers of neurolinguistic programming (NLP). NLP is concerned with the processes of communication, both verbal and nonverbal, between people. Holding that "the meaning of a communication is the response it elicits," NLP assumes that all, or certainly the great majority of, communications from one person to another are intended to elicit some sort of response. This is the outcome frame. Although in everyday conversation outcome frames are not usually consciously formulated, they nevertheless exist. Thus, if you say "Good morning" to a colleague you probably expect a similar reply; this is your outcome frame. How important it is to you to achieve your desired outcome will vary with the circumstances of the conversation or interaction.

Psychotherapy is an example of the process of communication, and one in which outcome frames are especially important. The "communications"—that is, all the verbal and nonverbal messages—that pass from therapists to their clients should be designed to elicit responses that assist the clients in achieving their objectives. Therapy is thus a meeting of therapist and client for the purpose of exchanging communications with a view to making changes. Such changes may be in the client's behavior or in his or her emotional state or relationships; in a family's way of functioning; or in a marital relationship. In such situations the establishment of agreed and clearly defined objectives is imperative, if time is not to be wasted. Therapist and client should both be clear about the objectives of the exercise. Jack did better than Jill because his outcome frame was better defined; that is, he knew exactly where he was going. Jill was just traveling hopefully. The same applies to psychotherapy.

There is nothing peculiar to the use of therapeutic metaphors that makes the setting of treatment objectives more important than it is in psychotherapy generally. Metaphorical methods, however, are usually employed as part of a strategic plan, and such a plan cannot be developed unless objectives have first been defined. It is therefore essential that we consider the establishing of objectives before we proceed any further.

Negotiating the objectives of treatment and reaching agreement may take a whole session, sometimes several, but the time usually proves to have been well spent. Even if agreement is never reached, so that treatment is not started, the time is not wasted; therapy embarked upon on the basis of misunderstood goals seldom produces results that are satisfactory to any of those concerned. The one possible exception to this is the long-running therapy in which some clients get to achieve "emotional growth" or "make gains," the "gains" never being defined in any precise way. Such therapy is rather like a fishing expedition in which the anglers have no idea what, if any, fish they are likely to catch, nor what they would do with any they did happen to land. This kind of therapy can be fun, of course, but metaphors are not needed to help define or achieve the goals of such therapy, since there are no defined goals.

DEFINING THE DESIRED STATE

It is helpful to obtain a clear and precise picture of the *desired state* that those coming for therapy wish to reach. Therapist and client should also define as precisely as possible how this desired state differs from the present state of affairs.

Many people come for therapy with negative goals. They want to feel less depressed, or to stop eating so much, or to stop smoking. Or they want their children to stop fighting, or their teenage daughter to cease refusing to eat the food they provide. These are all good reasons for seeking professional help—assuming that commonsense measures have proved ineffective—but they are not adequate as outcome frames. To put it another way, a description of a desired state requires more than a statement of what you *do not* want to be happening. A comprehensive picture of how you *do* want things to be is as useful to both client and therapist as is an architect's mental image of the building for which plans are about to be made.

So it may be useful to ask clients questions such as the following: If you don't want to feel depressed, how do you want to feel? (There are many alternatives to feeling depressed, and there may be times when it is appropriate to feel depressed; for example, people normally react with sadness to bereavements and losses and may feel guilty if they experience joy under such circumstances.) Or what will replace smoking, or eating, in your life? What will your children be doing if they are not fighting? What will serve the purpose that refusal to eat is serving in your daughter's life?

Such questions have often scarcely been considered by those

seeking therapy. Even when clients' goals are stated in positive terms, they are frequently vague and ill-defined, like Jill's instructions. Perhaps they want to "feel happier" or "have more energy" or "be able to decide what I want to do with my life." Such statements are all right as starting points for the discussion of treatment goals, but they are not in themselves adequate outcome frames. What does "feel happier" mean? Happier than what, or who? Under what circumstances does the person want to feel happier? How will client and therapist know that the desired degree of happiness has been achieved? And so on.

It is useful to get clients to describe, in as much detail as possible, how things will be when (and not if!) therapy is successfully concluded. (By talking about how things will be *when* therapy comes to an end, you embed in your statements the message that it will end successfully; but if you discuss how things will be *if* therapy reaches a successful conclusion, you are implying doubts about this, which is hardly the way to inspire confidence in your clients.)

Once the desired state has been described there are still some questions to be considered:

1. *Will there be any drawbacks to the desired state?* Will anything that at present offers gratification to someone concerned be lost and not replaced by a satisfactory alternative? For example, if the daughter who at present won't eat starts to eat the food her mother prepares, will this result in less closeness between mother and daughter, since there will be no further need for battles or discussions about the daughter's diet? Or will it mean less closeness between the parents, because they will not now need to spend long hours discussing their daughter's eating problem?

2. *What other consequences will follow once the changes the client seeks have occurred?* Careful consideration of how things will be for those involved when the specified changes have been made may lead to second thoughts. This in turn may lead to further modification of the objectives.

3. *What has so far stopped the client from making the changes sought?* This question is closely related to the foregoing ones, but asking it in this way places the issue of what is causing the symptoms to continue in a different perspective.

4. *Under what circumstances are the changes desired?* The desired new behaviors should be put into context. Most symptoms have value in some circumstances. Thus there are times when it is appropriate to refuse food, or to get angry, or to feel tired, or to be undecided about something. Thus it is worthwhile to get people to define exactly the situations in which they want the desired changes to be manifest and those in which they do not.

5. *How quickly do the clients want to change?* This is a useful thing to know, but it is also a good question to ask because of the statement embedded in it, namely, that change *will* occur if therapy is undertaken. By asking such a question the issue of whether the changes are possible is, by implication, dismissed and replaced by that of how quickly they should, and will, occur.

INTERMEDIATE AND FINAL GOALS

Sometimes it is helpful to distinguish short-term from long-term goals. Psychotherapy has been likened to traveling through the jungle, in which it is at times impossible to see your final objective and where you cannot survey, from your starting point, the route that will get you there most quickly and easily. While you need to know where you want to end up—otherwise you will wander aimlessly until you die of starvation or some creature eats you—it is often best to plan your journey in stages. A good way to proceed is to climb a tree, survey your route to the next landmark—probably another large tree—and then repeat the exercise as often as necessary until you reach your objective.

Psychotherapy, too, is often best approached in stages. Intermediate goals, equivalent to the trees the jungle traveler climbs to survey the next stage of the journey, may need to be set and achieved along the way. Each one of these is an opportunity to review progress and perhaps even to set a new course. The "jungle" metaphor, or any other metaphor that addresses the issue of proceeding on a journey by stages, may be used to explain this process to clients. The intermediate goals do not always have to be made explicit to the clients. Other metaphors may be used to help clients achieve small steps along the journey through the jungle.

USING METAPHOR TO HELP CLIENTS DEFINE THE CHANGES THEY SEEK

For therapists who believe that the setting of well-defined objectives is important, metaphorical methods offer a way of enabling people to prepare for therapy. Stories such as the following can be helpful in situations in which a straightforward explanation of the need to prepare objectives and review available resources proves insufficient.

> Norman, a man who was well skilled with his hands, wanted to build a garden shed. He went to a store that sold materials and supplies for the "do-it-yourself" market and asked for advice. The salesman Norman spoke to asked him a lot of questions, many of which he could not answer immediately. He wanted to know what kinds of things Norman planned to keep in the shed, how big it should be, on what sort of ground it was to be built and with what materials, what kind of floor Norman wanted it to have, what tools and equipment Norman already had at home and, finally, how much he could afford to spend on the shed.
>
> Norman realized that he needed to give a lot more thought to his project than he had done so far. First, he gathered together all the items he intended to keep in the shed, including his lawn mower, electric hedge-clipper and wheelbarrow, a number of garden tools, the fertilizer spreader and a couple of bags of fertilizer, his children's bicycles, some flower pots and seed boxes, and sundry smaller items. He was now able to estimate the size of shed he would need.
>
> Next Norman assembled all his wood-working and other

tools; these had been scattered in various parts of the house, and some had not been used for years. Indeed, he was surprised by some of his finds—tools he had long forgotten acquiring. The total was impressive, and it seemed as if Norman might have just about all the equipment he needed.

Norman now examined carefully the site where he planned to erect the shed. It was a damp area and it seemed safer to plan to have a wooden floor raised up, perhaps on concrete blocks, above ground level.

Finally Norman reviewed his financial situation; the salesman had given him a rough idea of what sheds made of different materials would cost and it seemed that he would be able to afford a cedarwood shed, which was what he had originally hoped to build.

Norman now had a pretty clear idea of what the shed he was going to build would look like, the work that would be involved in constructing it, and what it would cost in time and money. He decided to go ahead with it, and was ready to return, properly prepared, to the store to buy the materials he needed, to receive instructions and a plan of how to build the shed, and to purchase those few additional tools he required.

MOTIVATING CLIENTS

Closely related to the setting of objectives is the matter of motivation. Some people do not believe they can achieve the changes they truly desire. Some even come to therapists with the expectation that there will be no change! Beware the client who comes saying, "I just want someone to talk to," unless of course you are short of clients and need to keep the few you have attending indefinitely! You may need to help such people understand human beings' enormous potential for change before they can be engaged effectively in therapy.

Ferris (1980) quotes an interview with Lewis Thomas, in which Thomas talks about a beetle, the "Mimosa Girdler":

> The reason I like her so much is she's a good example of planning ahead, of real forethought in a creature that ob-

viously can't have much of a central nervous system. She
is attracted, first off, to mimosa trees. Doesn't live on any
other tree. She climbs up the mimosa trunk, goes out on a
limb, and cuts a longitudinal slit with her mandible, then
lays eggs in the slit, which almost immediately heals over
so that it can't be seen. She then goes back onto the limb
and spends a couple of hours digging a girdle around the
limb. It cuts the circulation off. She departs. The limb dies.
The next wind could break it off. And after it falls, the larvae
can now hatch, because they're in deadwood. And the cycle
begins again. Now, how did evolution achieve these two
separate and—when you think about it, or when she thinks
about it—quite unrelated acts of behavior? It looks as though
it's really been thought out. She wants to lay her eggs in
the mimosa because it's somehow attractive. They can't live
in live wood, and the nicest way to kill wood is to girdle it.
(p. 128).

Madanes (1981), in her book, *Strategic Family Therapy*, comments
thus on the above story: ''What could be the complexities and
mysteries of the way humans plan ahead if the little beetle does
it with such sophistication!'' (p. 222).

(There are other uses for the story of this beetle. Indeed,
Madanes uses it as a metaphor for a system that is stuck in one
pattern of interaction; the beetle has a plan, to be sure, but it can
only follow that plan, just as individuals in family systems sometimes continue following a particular pattern of behavior, even
though that pattern may have outlived its usefulness or may
never have been an especially good one. Unlike the little beetle,
though, human beings have enormous potential for learning from
their experiences and for changing their patterns of behavior—
hence their remarkable dominance on this planet.)

Metaphors can help motivate clients to decide whether they
want therapy at all. A couple with severe marital problems had
attended several times but seemed unable to make up their minds
whether they wanted therapy for their problems or whether they
wished to separate. A simple analogy helped them decide. Their
situation, I told them, was like that of a couple of people stumbling

along a trail in a forest. They had come to a place where the trail divided; in one direction the trail was labeled "therapy," the other route was labeled "separation." But, I pointed out, they need not take *either* route; a third possibility was to take a middle course and fight their way through the undergrowth of the forest. The wife telephoned a few days later to say that she and her husband had agreed they wanted marital therapy and requested an appointment.

SUMMARY

Psychotherapy, like most other human activities, is more likely to be successful if it starts with clear goals, and if some time and effort are spent in planning how these are to be achieved. It is therefore important to begin therapy with well-defined objectives that are agreed upon between therapist and client.

The *desired state* is that which, when achieved, will constitute a completely satisfactory therapy result. It should be stated in positive, rather than negative, terms; that is, it should describe how things *will* be at the successful conclusion of treatment, rather than how they will *not* be.

Metaphors can assist both in motivating clients to become actively involved in defining the desired outcomes—for example, through telling stories about endeavors that failed because they were embarked upon without properly defined objectives—and in the actual process of developing the objectives. They can also inspire people who feel their situation is hopeless, or almost so, to believe that change for the better is possible.

A PRACTICAL EXERCISE

Gregory, a young man of superior intelligence and good looks, has for the third time dropped out of a university course because he found it "boring" and has gotten into angry clashes with his teachers, most of whom he considers to be fools. He has come to see you only because he was urged to do so by the student health service physician. He can't see that psychotherapy is likely to achieve anything much, and you gain the impression that his opinion of therapists is not much higher than his opinion of his teachers.

Devise a metaphorical story that might help Gregory understand how therapy could lead to some useful outcomes.

5

Metaphors for Developmental Problems

THE PHILIPPINE EAGLE

The Philippine eagle lays only one egg each breeding season, so its offspring is very precious. The mother eagle looks after her eaglet with great care, feeding it regularly until it is strong enough to fend for itself.

The big problem the mother is faced with as the eaglet grows up is that of knowing when the young bird can indeed take care of itself. If she allows it to leave the eyrie before it can make a kill or defend itself, it will perish, either from starvation or as a result of an attack by another predator. If she waits too long the best time for learning to make a kill will have passed. So the process of handing over responsibility to the young bird, and of teaching it to survive in the world, is a delicate one.

In practice eagles usually survive. The delicate adjustment of roles occurs at just the right speed to give the young bird the best chance in life. The mother eagle watches carefully for all the signs that will tell her that the young bird has developed sufficiently to be allowed out of the eyrie. Perhaps the eaglet also has a feeling that tells it when it's strong enough to fend for itself. We don't know precisely how the process occurs. Probably instinct has a lot to do with it. And we can only wonder about the heart-searching that perhaps goes on within both mother eagle and her eaglet while we admire the way, time and again, they make the right judgments and the species survives.

DEVELOPMENT AND DEVELOPMENTAL REFRAMING

Life is a long process of development, from conception to the grave. Human beings remain dependent proportionately longer than any other animal species, presumably because they have more to learn before they can cope successfully with the adult world. The decisions the eagle and her eaglet have to make are faced many times, and in many forms, by human parents and their children.

Many of the clinical problems with which therapists are confronted are problems of development. While they do not always present as such, it is sometimes helpful to reframe them in developmental terms. Coppersmith (1981) has discussed the clinical uses of this process of *developmental reframing*. For example, when parents complain of the behavior of a young adolescent, developmental reframing would involve telling the family, in essence, that the young person is neither mad nor bad, but rather is behaving "young" for his or her age. When the complained-of behavior is seen as immature, rather than due to some deep psychological disturbance or, perhaps, some form of original sin, it usually comes to be regarded in a different light. Not only is the young person challenged to prove the therapist wrong by behaving in a more mature fashion, but the parents, and other family members, are likely to alter their attitudes toward the problem. In helping them do this, and in the reframing process itself, metaphors can be useful.

Developmental reframing does itself involve the use of metaphor. When a 14-year-old is described as being an 8-year-old, as may happen when this therapeutic device is used, the therapist does not of course mean that the adolescent is actually 8; using this description is just a metaphorical way of saying something about the subject's level of emotional development.

AN APPROACH TO DEVELOPMENTAL PROBLEMS

How can therapists help people who experience difficulty when facing the challenge of a developmental hurdle? The first step of course is to assess the clinical situation carefully and to establish the desired *outcome frame*, as discussed in Chapter 4. How to assess individual development, and what to expect at different ages, will not be discussed here. An outline of normal development, and of how to carry out the psychiatric assessment of children and adolescents, is to be found in *Basic Child Psychiatry* (Barker, 1983). Fuller accounts of human development can be found in psychology texts. Most therapists who are considering the use of therapeutic metaphors to assist clients in overcoming developmental hurdles will be familiar with the stages of human development.

Family development is important too. This also has been discussed elsewhere (Barker, 1981b), but the main points are worth mentioning here, because metaphors can help families surmount developmental hurdles that are presenting them with difficulty.

Barnhill and Longo (1978) define nine "transition points" that must be passed as families move from stage to stage in their development. Barnhill and Longo took the eight stages of family development described by Duvall (1977) and examined the transitions that have to occur as one stage succeeds another. They described the transition points between the stages (see Table 3), the numbers referring to Duvall's stages; thus I-II refers, for example, to the transition from being a childless married couple (Duvall's first stage) to being a childbearing family (Duvall's second stage).

Family development and individual development are not, of course, separate processes. Negotiating each of the above transition points entails change not only in the family system but in the individuals concerned. Metaphors can assist with both processes.

Table 3
Transition Points in Family Development

0–I *Commitment* of the couple to each other.

I–II *Developing new, parent roles*, as husband and wife become father and mother.

II–III *Accepting the new personality*, as the child grows up.

III–IV *Introducing the child to institutions outside the family*; for example school, church, scouts, sports, and other youth activities.

IV–V *Accepting adolescence*, with its changed roles and the parents' need to come to terms with the rapid social and sexual changes occurring in sons and daughters.

V–VI *Experimenting with independence*, a task carried out by the young person and permitted, even encouraged, by the parents.

VI–VII *Preparation to launch*, the acceptance by the parents of their child's independence, and the young person's preparation for an independent life outside the family of origin.

VII–VIII *Letting go–facing each other again*, the point at which the parents have finished child-rearing and face each other as husband and wife alone again.

VIII–IX *Accepting retirement and/or old age*, with the changed lifestyle involved.

Source: Adapted from Barnhill & Longo, 1978.

Life around us is rich in sources from which we may construct metaphors relating to developmental issues. Both the animal and the plant kingdoms are characterized by processes of growth and reproduction, followed by decline, after which a new generation takes the place of the old. The biblical parable of the sower is an excellent example. The story tells of a sower scattering grain, some of which fell on the path, some on rocky ground, some among thorn bushes, and some in good soil. Only the latter took root satisfactorily. In the Bible this story is used to illustrate the responses of different people to Christ's teaching, but it could be used to illustrate commitment or the lack of it (only when the seed and the right environment came together could there be commitment and development). Or the relationship between the soil and the seed could be used as a metaphor for the relationship between parents and their children, who must be nourished much as seeds are by the soil in which they grow. What happened to the seed that fell among thorns could be a metaphor for the experience of children brought up in unfavorable circumstances of one sort or another.

So many aspects of farming are analogous to child-rearing that the agricultural scene offers rich opportunities for the construction of metaphors relating to developmental issues. Sometimes things go well for the farmer. The sun shines when sunshine is needed and the rains come when they are required. The soil is fertile, the seed planted is of good quality and the right strain for the prevailing conditions, and the farm machinery functions without a hitch. Sometimes things go wrong, maybe slightly wrong, maybe drastically so. The problem may lie in the weather conditions, the soil, the seed, the machinery, the paid help, workers' wage demands, market conditions and the price of grain, or any combination of these things. Over the centuries, though, farmers have learnt to deal with their problems in a variety of ingenious ways.

Child rearing and family life, too, may go smoothly. But they may also present minor difficulties or even be subject to drastic reverses and setbacks. Whatever the situation, it is usually possible to find, in what may happen on a farm, some isomorphic metaphorical equivalent. And among the ways farmers use to cope with their difficulties, there are usually some that have metaphorical relevance to family life.

COMMITMENT METAPHORS

When clients' problems appear to be based on a lack of commitment—as with married couples whose commitment to each other is weak or ambivalent—therapeutic metaphors cannot be expected to create commitment that does not exist. Metaphors can help, however, by pointing out, in an indirect way, the nature of the problems. Sometimes they can also suggest possible solutions.

Peter was a skilled cabinetmaker, and Paul had worked in the construction industry doing a variety of carpenter's jobs. As both were unemployed, they decided to start a joint venture making and selling kitchen furniture. They had been friends for several years, so they felt sure they would have no difficulty getting along together in business.

At first the joint venture went well, but it wasn't long before disagreements between the partners surfaced. These led to increasing tension and quite vicious arguments between the friends. Each had his own idea about how the business should be run, what products they should make, and how they should market them. Each also seemed to have a need to have his view prevail. Neither was willing to give in to the other, even for the sake of the business, though they both knew that in the competitive field in which they were engaged they had to work together if they were to have any hope of success.

What started out as a happy arrangement, with high hopes for a long and productive working relationship on the part of both partners, soon deteriorated into an unhappy one marked by a succession of acrimonious disputes. Worse, the venture proved financially disappointing too. The sales and cash flow predictions with which they started were just not being met.

In desperation, Peter and Paul went to see a business consultant, to seek advice on how they could save their business. The consultant listened patiently to what each had to say, examined their books, and discussed their plans for the development of their business and the marketing of their products. After he had done all this he gave them his opinion.

"You both seem to be highly competent people in your fields," he said. "You're making good quality products and they're competitively priced, but you don't seem to be able to agree about which products to concentrate on, who to try to sell them to, or how to market them. You've assumed that because you've been good friends for several years this would be sufficient to create a good working business relationship. Your friendship can certainly help, but it's not enough. There must be a commitment to the business relationship and an agreement about what the nature of the business is to be. Of course this can follow discussion, even heated discussion, but until the business relationship becomes more important than your personal views, which then become secondary to the interests of the business, you're unlikely to have much success. If you can't reach agreement on precisely the type of business you want to commit yourselves to running, I'd suggest you go your separate ways.''

The above might be a useful metaphor for some married couples having difficulty making a commitment to being married and in disagreement about what they want the nature of their marital relationship to be. It should be modified to make it isomorphic—that is equivalent in metaphorical form—with the actual state of the marriage. Thus, for example, if the marital partners had known each other only a few weeks, the therapist would need to alter the story to reflect this fact. If there were no violent arguments, but instead one partner had become depressed or had taken to sulking and refusing to discuss issues while the other responded in some other way, the "business relationship" could be modified accordingly.

The story could also be expanded to suggest possible solutions other than the fairly general ones included in the version above. The consultant might suggest *how* the business partners might go about resolving their differences. Or the story might continue to describe how they *did*—perhaps by the use of their own personal resources—reach agreement on how to work together in harmony, so that their business flourished and lasted many happy and prosperous years.

Yet another option is to describe two joint ventures, both in trouble. In one story the business partners resolve their difficulties in a way analogous to one the therapist sees as open to the marital partners; in the other they agree on an amicable dissolution of the business relationship. This would give the partners a choice of courses.

PARENTING METAPHORS

The story of the Philippine eagle is but one example of a parenting metaphor derived from the animal kingdom. In the form used above it addresses primarily the "preparations to launch" stage of family development. In this form, or one similar to it, it is often useful in helping families in which parents and their adolescent children are having difficulty separating out. For parents, it defines the task they are faced with in letting their child go forth into the world as an independent person, and it also says something about how to judge when the time is right to do this. For adolescents, it sets out in metaphorical form the developmental task they have to carry out and it tells them too how to decide whether they are ready to do this.

The case of the Philippine eagle, or other examples from the animal kingdom, may be used to assist families who are having difficulty at earlier stages in their development. To go back, for example, to Barnhill and Longo's preceding stage, "experimenting with independence," the story could be modified to describe how the mother eagle allows her offspring short periods away from the eyrie, as it first learns to fly. Her anxiety about letting the young bird out of her sight, even for short periods, could be described (if this is isomorphic with the real-life situation of the family), with an explanation that this is an essential stage in the young bird's development if it is ever to learn to survive in the forest. The point might also be made that the mother keeps a discreet eye on the eaglet while it is doing its experimenting, so as to make a skilled judgment about just how closely to supervise the bird at each particular stage of its development.

This may be a good point at which to consider whether it matters how factually accurate the therapist's account of the subject of the metaphor is. Does one have to know a lot, for example, about Philippine eagles? Does there even have to be such a thing as a Philippine eagle? I believe that it is not necessary to be at all times scientifically or factually correct, at least when describing things about which the family do not have expert knowledge. But if the therapist can be factually accurate, so much the better.

If you are speaking to people who have, or may have, expert knowledge in the area—for example, someone with a degree in zoology if a metaphor concerning the behavior of animals is to be used—it is well to have your facts right. An alternative, however, is to tell the story "in quotes." That is to say, you start by saying something like, "A friend of mine was telling me the other day about the Philippine eagle." If you are especially doubtful about the accuracy or veracity of what you are going to say, you may wish to add such a statement as, "I'm not sure whether what he said was absolutely accurate, but I thought it was quite interesting anyway." Saying that you thought the story was interesting, incidentally, is another way of suggesting something indirectly to your clients. Unconsciously the client's response may be, "If the therapist thought it was interesting, or learnt something from it, perhaps I will too."

Other phrases that can be used to introduce animal stories, or fairy tales of one's own construction, are, "That reminds me of a story a friend of mine used to tell his kids," or "I once knew a little girl who was fascinated by a story about. . . . " The story can then be told without any pretence that it is true or that the therapist believes it. Yet another option is to tell the story to the child or children in the family, but in the presence of the parents. This defines it as a children's story, and not necessarily literally true, while at the same time the parents hear it and are provided with the opportunity, at an unconscious level, to use it for their own purposes.

Metaphors from the animal kingdom can be helpful in treating families in which there are difficulties in early stages of the child-rearing process. Parents who have difficulty in accepting the personality, behavior, or appearance of their young child can be told stories about animals who were "surprised" by the appearance or behavior of their offspring, but later found that the surprising or unexpected features had value in ways they had not imagined possible. While not all parents will accept such stories, especially if they presuppose feelings and thoughts on the part of the animals, it is nevertheless remarkable how often such metaphors can be used, once rapport has been established and when the stories are introduced in the correct way.

In this context the story of the Ugly Duckling can be useful. It is almost a universal metaphor for the situation of children who are perceived, both by others and by themselves, as imperfect but have the potential (as of course all children do) to change and become something different and better.

Developmental issues can also be addressed by telling stories about other families—perhaps families the therapist has treated previously—who have been confronted by similar, or at least analogous, problems. In doing this there may be less of a "metaphorical disguise"; that is, it may be obvious to the client family that a solution to their problems, or a new view of them, is being offered. The disguise can be thickened, however, by altering the nature of the problem, the number, ages, and/or sexes of the children, or other aspects of the family under treatment, when constructing the metaphor.

If you use stories about other families, it is essential that they be so disguised as to be quite unrecognizable. In small communities especially it is often widely known who is attending therapy, or which families or individuals are having problems, and any suspicion that a therapist is telling some clients about others could obviously have serious repercussions. As a migrant to Canada from the British Isles, I often preface such stories with phrases like, "When I worked in Scotland, before I came to Canada, I saw a family that. . . . " This places the story in a quite different context and makes it clear that no neighbors of the family in therapy are being discussed.

HELPING CLIENTS SURMOUNT DEVELOPMENTAL BLOCKS

Sometimes a family or an individual is struggling unsuccessfully to use methods that were useful at an earlier stage in dealing with current issues. Adolescents, for example, often fail to respond to parental approaches that are highly effective for prepubertal children. Some parents continue to give their toddlers the same constant attention and handle them as protectively as they did—appropriately—when they were infants a few months of age. Parents of grown-up, married children with families of

their own sometimes cannot resist the temptation to continue giving their adult offspring advice, advice that is often unwelcome
and thus counterproductive.

Metaphors for such situations abound, for the world is full of
people using outdated technologies, or attempting to solve problems by means that no longer work because of changed circumstances. Readers will be able to think of their own examples:
Firms that fail to replace old machinery with more modern equipment; the worker promoted from the factory floor who fails to
learn to dress, act, and talk like an executive; or the fisherman
who continues to try and catch fish using the same type of fly
he was successful with yesterday, even though conditions today
are different.

Another approach to these problems, one that is a little less
indirect, is to talk about how people sometimes do, surprisingly,
continue to use child-rearing methods that are proving ineffective. A family may be offered something along these lines.

> One of the things that sometimes surprises me is the way
> some people keep on trying things that don't work. I often
> wonder why this is. Sometimes it seems to be because in
> the past the things they are trying have worked and they
> have a sort of feeling that they still should. I must admit that
> at times I can't myself understand why they don't work, but
> presumably the situation must have changed in some way
> so that what was successful before isn't any more.

> It certainly can be a bit of a problem for people to know
> what to do in this sort of situation. I guess you have a choice
> between trying to figure out why the old methods no longer
> work, or just leaving that as a mystery and trying something
> new. A lot of people seem to find it best to move along and
> try something new, once they realize that they are fighting
> a lost cause in attempting to get their old methods to work.
> Sometimes I tell them I really don't know what will be the
> best method of handling the situation. I just suggest they
> try something—anything—different.

This sort of approach has a number of advantages. I am of
course addressing the family, or the parent or parents, meta-

phorically, telling them something about their situation while ostensibly talking about other families. I am also sharing with the parents their feelings of mystification about the failure of their methods of handling their children—or whatever the problems may be. Empathy, and a desire to try what the therapist suggests, are sometimes increased when the therapist avoids playing the role of ''expert,'' but instead joins the family in their sense of frustration.

METAPHORS FOR LATER LIFE

The elderly and retired, as well as younger people who, because of illness or an acquired handicap, have to modify their lifestyles, can sometimes be helped by the use of metaphors. Finding different uses for things, discovering previously unrealized potential in people or objects, and recycling are all commonplace aspects of present-day culture. References to such phenomena can be made when treating people faced with big changes in their life situations. Such references are often best slipped in as brief anecdotes, or just as items mentioned casually or incidentally in the course of conversation. They nevertheless suggest to clients that the changes could be opportunities for growth; they may also promote the discovery of new ways of using people's talents and potential.

When I was a child, I lived for a time on a farm in the English midlands. In those days, during World War II, electric power lines had not yet reached this area. The farmer cultivated quite a large acreage of hops, a profitable crop in a country where people drink as much hop-flavored beer as the British do. Once picked, hops must be dried in kilns, the operation of which needs electricity. The farmers in the area therefore generated their own electricity, in most cases using diesel engines. The farmer on whose farm I lived did indeed have a diesel engine, but he also used a farm tractor, which was equipped with a drive wheel to assist in the generation of electricity. This tractor had been retired from work in the fields. There were problems with its wheels, tires, and steering, but it now had a new and valuable function as a generator of electricity.

It may be that not all old people or people who have suffered strokes or heart problems will want to be compared to farm tractors. This metaphor nevertheless has been used with success. Some people, of course, can accept this sort of message presented in a direct, logically argued form. But many cannot. For them, metaphorical presentation of the message is an alternative. The message is offered to the unconscious mind (the "right brain" in Watzlawick's, 1978, terminology), while the conscious mind (or "left brain") remains unaware of what is going on; it "thinks" the conversation is about farm machinery!

Therapists will naturally have their own experiences which they can build into metaphors they are comfortable about using; perhaps there are none who have shared the particular experience recounted above and who thus would want to use this story exactly as it stands. Metaphors do not always have to be drawn from the therapist's own life experiences, however.

KID GLOVES

Coppersmith (in press) offers us a beautiful illustration of the use of a ritual and a metaphorical object in helping a mother and her daughter surmount a developmental hurdle. The ritual was designed to further the process of normalizing the relationship between the mother and her young adult daughter, who had earlier been diagnosed as a "paranoid schizophrenic." The relationship had been more that of custodian and patient.

> They were instructed to go shopping together, which they heartily enjoyed, and to find the most elegant, most expensive pair of kid gloves possible. When they returned home, the mother, with the daughter watching, was to soak the gloves in a bowl of water and put the bowl, gloves and all, in the freezer. She was then instructed to continue to treat her daughter with kid gloves when she needed to, but only *after* she had removed the gloves from the freezer and let

them thaw out. Mother and daughter did the ritual with great care and lots of laughter. The daughter continued to grow in responsible action and the mother stopped being afraid of her or of making appropriate demands on her. The kid gloves stayed in the freezer and became part of the family's "inner language." (Coppersmith, in press)

SUMMARY

Many of the problems with which therapists are confronted are problems of development. This is often not apparent to the clients, however, and metaphors may be used to reframe problems in developmental terms.

Metaphors may suggest the need for change, for example, in child-rearing patterns or in the amount of responsibility an individual accepts at different stages of the family or the individual life cycle.

The animal and plant kingdoms demonstrate the processes of growth, development, decline, and the succession by another generation in many and diverse ways; they therefore offer a rich variety of metaphorical illustrations of the various issues that arise in the course of individual and family development.

Metaphors may be used to promote family development at any stage. Metaphors about commitment can assist newly married couples who are having difficulty making the commitment to each other that is needed for a sound marriage; stories about family life in the animal kingdom, or about other families that have overcome developmental difficulties may help families having problems at later stages in the family life cycle. Stories about changes in function and the discovery of new uses for things and hitherto unrecognized potentials may help those facing the adjustments of later life.

A PRACTICAL EXERCISE

Jeanette K. is 13 and has recently started to develop quite rapidly, both physically and in her interests outside the family and home. She is the eldest of her parents' three children. For the last six months or so there have been repeated episodes of conflict, of increasing severity, between the parents and Jeanette. Mr. and Mrs. K. are very distressed that their previously compliant and well-behaved daughter has become, as they put it, "unmanageable" and a constant source of worry to them. They fear she is "getting in with the wrong crowd" and that she may be on drugs, but every attempt they make to talk to her about their concerns is met with denial by Jeanette that there is any problem. She then usually gets angry, shouts at them, and threatens to leave home.

The parents have received counseling at a local family services agency. The counselor aimed to give Mr. and Mrs. K. an understanding of the normal developmental processes of adolescence and some guidance as to how to help their daughter through this stage of development. Jeanette refused to attend, however, and the situation has continued to deteriorate. Despite what they have been told, the parents still believe the problem is Jeanette's and that there is something seriously wrong with her.

Devise a metaphorical approach to this family developmental problem, designed to reframe the problem as a parent/child relationship difficulty and to offer both Jeanette and the parents ways of resolving their dilemma.

6

Metaphors for Conduct Disorders and Other Behavioral Problems

Rosalie was nearly ten. Three weeks before her birthday the family's cat was run over by a car and killed. But Rosalie had always wanted a dog and, with the cat dead and her birthday coming up, this seemed to her an ideal moment to persuade her parents to give her one.

The parents had never been keen on having a dog. They considered dogs messy creatures, difficult to train, needing a lot of care and presenting a problem when their owners want to go away on holiday. Despite their reservations, however, Rosalie succeeded in convincing them that they should buy her a dog. She promised faithfully to look after it properly.

The dog, a Scottish Terrier puppy, arrived, and Rosalie was ecstatic. She named the puppy Joshua, Josh for short. He proved affectionate and playful, but unruly and destructive. As the weeks passed it also became clear that he was

90

not responding to the family's attempts to house train him. Rosalie did her best, helped by a book on training dogs, and her parents did their best to help her. But Josh continued to make puddles and messes around the house, and his general behavior didn't become noticeably less unruly. The parents labelled him "hyperactive" and began to wonder if there was something constitutionally wrong with him. Rosalie always defended Josh vehemently when any accusations were made against him, but sometimes she too secretly wondered whether there might not be something wrong with him.

The situation got no better. Josh was becoming more and more like a wild animal, roaming the house and dealing out chaos and destruction at every turn. Rosalie's parents started arguing about him. Her mother was fast becoming convinced that Josh would have to go. She was the one who did most of the cleaning up after him, but despite her efforts the furniture was beginning to deteriorate as Josh pawed it, scratched it, and walked all over it with his muddy feet. The father, on the other hand, couldn't find it in his heart to get rid of Josh, knowing how much Rosalie loved him. This situation led to increasingly strong disagreements in the family and bitter disputes about how best to train Joshua.

Eventually the family decided to take Josh to the vet to find out if there was something wrong with him that made it impossible to train him successfully. The vet examined the protesting Josh and pronounced him a normal healthy puppy. He could see no reason why Joshua should not be successfully trained. He recommended a dog trainer to the family. But the parents were far from convinced that there was nothing wrong with Joshua, and the dog trainer's fees were high. So they hesitated a while before taking up the vet's suggestion.

Two more weeks passed and Joshua's behavior continued to deteriorate. The family were getting into even bigger fights about the dog, so they finally decided to consult the trainer. He listened carefully to what the family told him about Josh and how they had tried to train him; he observed Josh's behavior and reactions to the family's attempts to control him. Then he gave them his opinion.

"I can't see any reason why your dog cannot be trained and become a well-behaved and obedient animal," he said. "It will take a bit of time as he has a fair amount of unlearning to do. He's certainly a very active puppy and training him will be hard work. But if you stick together and come and consult with me regularly for a time, I'm sure things will work out all right in the end."

Rosalie was overjoyed at this opinion. The parents weren't so sure they believed it. Joshua had been so utterly unresponsive to their love, care, and efforts to train him that they still thought there was something radically wrong with him. In desperation, though, they decided to give the trainer's recommendations a fair trial and they worked hard doing so. Greatly to their surprise, things quite quickly started to improve. Joshua stopped wetting the floor and he even started to sit when told! Encouraged by this, the family kept their subsequent appointments with the trainer, whose advice seemed sound after all.

The improvement in Joshua's behavior continued until he became, even for Rosalie's mother, a pleasure to have about the house.

"It's amazing," she told Rosalie's father one day, "what training and a different environment can do."

CONDUCT DISORDERS IN CHILDREN

Epidemiological studies (Rutter, Tizard & Whitmore, 1970; Rutter, 1973) have shown that conduct disorders are the commonest of the psychiatric disorders of childhood. Their causes are usually multiple and complex, and they are often associated with serious family and/or social problems (Barker, 1983). Such problems can be hard to resolve, so that treatment can present great challenges. In many instances conduct disorders in children are but one aspect of a pattern of poor family functioning. Such patterns themselves make therapy difficult, because they are often characterized by attitudes of indifference on the part of family members, a lack of commitment to therapy, and difficulty in using some types of therapy.

Despite their high prevalence, and the serious implications for the future life and wellbeing of those who display antisocial behavior in childhood (Robins, 1966), there is little consensus on how best to treat conduct disorders, especially in adolescence. Both Romig (1978) and Shamsie (1981), in their reviews of the subject, comment on the general lack of success, especially in the treatment of the more severely antisocial adolescents. Shamsie concludes that "the treatments available to help antisocial adolescents are remarkably unsuccessful" (p. 362). He points out that there is some evidence to suggest that treatment is more likely to be successful if antisocial behavior in adolescents is regarded as "a problem arising from the lack of socialization . . . caused by inadequate attempts to teach socialization . . . or by a defect in the learning ability" (p. 362) of the subjects concerned. Shamsie (1981) also points out that adolescents displaying antisocial behavior do not usually express any discomfort, nor do they seem to want any intrapsychic problems solved. This perhaps points to the desirability of seeing these problems as family ones, rather than as disorders of the children themselves.

The family is the institution in which the process of socialization normally occurs. Careful attention should therefore be given to the families of children with conduct disorders. The therapist must try and understand how it is that socialization of the child or children has failed.

It is true that the failure of socialization usually has multiple causes. It may not simply be a result of the way the parents have brought up the child. Some children have "difficult" temperaments (Thomas & Chess, 1977), while the wider social environment—for example, a "delinquent" neighborhood or a difficult school situation—can also have adverse effects. Nevertheless the family environment is usually the most important factor, as well as being the one most open to change; moreover, the more difficult the child's temperament, or the more adverse the social factors, the greater the need for a stable home environment and skilled parenting.

Early assessment and treatment almost certainly improve the chances of successful treatment of children with conduct disorders. The difficult adolescents referred to by Romig (1978),

Shamsie (1981) and others (for example, Barker, 1978, Rae-Grant, 1978, and Warren, 1978), appear mostly to be the products of many years during which the development of the child's social behavior has been going awry. Once a full-blown picture of anti-social behavior in adolescence has emerged, treatment usually presents a big challenge.

METAPHORS FOR THE FAMILIES OF CHILDREN
WITH CONDUCT DISORDERS

The use of metaphor, like that of other therapy techniques, requires, first, a careful assessment of the family and the setting of therapeutic objectives, as discussed in Chapter 4. Metaphorical methods are certainly no panacea for these often difficult problems. Moreover, their use cannot be considered a separate therapeutic modality; and we are certainly not discussing a distinct school of psychotherapy. Metaphorical approaches represent rather a collection of techniques that may be used in the course of many types of therapy. Since these can be particularly difficult cases to treat successfully, we need to have available every resource that may be helpful. In my experience, metaphor can be helpful.

In the following sections we will consider some of the ways metaphorical techniques may be of value when the families of children with antisocial behavior are being assessed and treated: Motivating families to become involved in the study and assessment of the problem; motivating family members to become involved in treatment; reframing the problems of conduct disordered children as disorders of socialization; other types of reframing; and suggesting new approaches and possible solutions to specific problems.

Motivating Families to Become Involved in the Assessment Process

Many families are reluctant to see the antisocial behavior of one member as having anything much to do with the rest of the family group. Sometimes a straightforward explanation of the reasons why it is helpful to work with the whole family is enough to get everyone involved. In doing this it is usually best to refer to the family as part of the cure, not the cause of the problem. Sometimes, however, such explanations are insufficient and a metaphorical, or other indirect, approach is effective.

To motivate people to become involved in assessment or treatment, the therapist has the choice of either telling stories or anecdotes about other families that have come—or perhaps have declined to come—into assessment or treatment or of using metaphors from activities other than therapy. Stories about other families or clients may be real or constructed. I seldom create totally fictitious clients, but often use composite accounts of my work with several individuals or families. I always alter the facts (like age and sex of the children, occupation of the parents and other identifying data), both for ethical reasons and so as to make the story correspond, to a sufficient degree, with the actual situation of the clients being seen. Most important of all, of course, is to ensure that the metaphor has the effect of meeting the needs of the clients concerned.

How closely should a story about other clients resemble the situation of those to whom it is being told? This is a hard question. The answer depends on both the type of family and the clinical situation. Fortunately, therapists usually have the opportunity of telling a series of stories and observing the effects of each. This is one of the many advantages of the use of stories: several can be told, and as long as rapport is maintained with the family the therapist can continue until the desired therapeutic effect is obtained. By contrast, if families are told directly what the therapist would like them to do, or thinks they should do, and they decline the suggestion or refuse the advice, a state of confrontation has arisen that the therapist may find difficult to resolve.

When suggestions are put forward in metaphorical form, the response is often given nonverbally. Even when both verbal and nonverbal responses are made, the nonverbal ones are usually the more dependable as indicators of how the subjects really feel. The therapist should therefore be alert to the nonverbal informa-

tion that is being offered by clients and when necessary modify
the content of the metaphor according to responses observed (see
also Chapter 11).

When stories about other families are used as metaphors the
"metaphorical disguise" is usually quite thin. Most times the
clients realize consciously that they are being told something that
has a bearing on their participation in treatment, or whatever else
the issue may be. Yet to talk about other families, and how they
responded or behaved in analogous situations, sometimes seems
to enable clients to accept ideas that they are not willing to accept directly. We can assume that this approach tends to produce
unconscious change, as the clients are given no direct injunctions,
and therefore have nothing to resist at the conscious level. Referring again to Watzlawick's (1978) model, we may be by-passing
the left brain here and appealing directly to the right brain in
which emotional attitudes and feelings are presumably represented. Telling stories such as the following is also a way of in-
viting people to make changes—such as deciding to participate
in assessment or therapy—while at the same time not causing
them to feel pressured to make a decision.

The following story is an example of how a therapist may address issues such as we have been discussing. It is the sort of
thing that might be offered at the end of a session with a family
some of whose members are disinclined to return. It might also
be the subject of a telephone conversation with a reluctant family
member. Or it might be part of an individual interview with
someone who does not wish to become involved in family interviews. It was in fact addressed to a father who was reluctant
to come to a family assessment interview.

>   I remember a family I worked with before I came to this
> city. They were all very caring people, and the parents were
> deeply concerned about their 13-year-old daughter who had
> started running away and getting into trouble with the law.
> They also suspected that she was on drugs, though she
> denied it and the parents had no proof. There were two
> other children in the family, both girls and both older than

the daughter who was in trouble. Neither of them had been in trouble and the parents had no particular concerns about them.

As none of the other members of the family appeared to have any problems, the reasons for the daughter's behavior were a real puzzle to the family. Their family doctor suggested that they bring the daughter to see me, and she came to my office with her mother. I had long talks with both of them and at the end of it all I was as puzzled as the family. They seemed delightful people, and both mother and daughter appeared quite open in the interview situation. From what the mother told me it seemed also that the parents had handled their daughter's problem behavior quite sensibly; they hadn't over-reacted, they'd spent long hours discussing the problems with the daughter, trying to figure out what had gone wrong and what they could do about it, and they had imposed reasonable sanctions in response to the daughter's misdeeds, though these had not been effective.

In those days I didn't always ask the whole family to come when I first saw a child, as I do nowadays. But this time I felt I needed more information. Naturally I first thought of the father. So I called him up and said I needed his help. I asked him to bring the whole family, including the two other daughters, to see me. I said I thought probably he, and perhaps the other girls too, could help me understand the youngest daughter's problems. He wasn't too keen on the idea nor, he told me, would the other girls be. He was very busy at his work and therefore reluctant to take time off. He feared losing his job, a fear which I felt probably wasn't fully justified as he had a long and excellent work record with the same firm. The other girls were good students at school, they had exams coming up and didn't like missing school. I commented that this was interesting since Patricia, the problem child, was reported to have a negative attitude toward school and was not doing well there. Eventually, after a good deal of discussion, the father agreed to come and to bring the whole family.

I was quite new to family therapy in those days and I had a lot to learn. What surprised me was how much I learned from that first interview with the complete household. The father was a very perceptive person. He was able to tell me a lot about the relationship between Pat and her mother that I hadn't even guessed when I just saw the two of them. The other daughters, too, gave me much new information. Seeing them together made me realize how close they were emotionally. The mother had told me they were close, but it wasn't till I actually saw them, and how they interacted, that the nature of their relationship really hit me.

It was also only when I saw the whole family that I appreciated how different the two older girls were in looks compared to Patricia. They were both strikingly attractive blondes with slim figures, whereas Pat was a little overweight, had mousy-colored hair and an altogether less striking appearance. Though not ugly, she certainly wasn't as attractive as her sisters.

Seeing the whole family helped me a lot. The problem for me was to understand how, in what seemed a basically healthy, normal family, there could be one member with problems as serious as Patricia's.

Space does not permit a detailed examination of every metaphor quoted in this book. Moreover you will learn more by studying the metaphors yourself and working out their possible meanings than you will from having them explained each time. On this occasion, however, it may be worthwhile pointing out some features of the above account, which were designed to help a reluctant parent attend a family assessment, and to bring his two older daughters as well. The story also contains points of significance that are not listed below but that you might like to search for.

The family the anecdote speaks about are presented in a positive light. They were "very caring people" and the parents "were deeply concerned" about the daughter.

Most parents care deeply about their children and in the family with whom this story was used there was no reason to suppose that this was not the case. The story also describes the parents as "delightful people" who had handled the situation sensibly, doing their best to resolve it with their own resources.

As a rule it is best to present people in a positive light when they are referred to metaphorically. Most parents do their best. The therapist should assume that they have been using the resources available to them as well as they know how, however disastrous the results may have been. Sometimes, though, clients present who are feeling guilty, perhaps about how they have cared for a child. In these circumstances it may be helpful to refer to the guilt feelings in the metaphor.

The therapist was puzzled too.   It can often be helpful to operate from either a "one-down" position or at least from one in which the therapist is no more than the family's equal in understanding the case. In the story above the therapist told the father that he needed the latter's help. Here was the "expert" asking the father for assistance! I did not say anything about the father being to blame, even to the smallest extent, for the problems. The parents, especially the father, in the family in which this story was used had the reputation for being suspicious and hostile towards "experts" who tried to give them advice or thought they knew better than the parents. The story took this into account.

The therapist was just starting to work with families when the events in the anecdote occurred, and had a lot to learn.   The therapist is thus presented as being open to new knowledge and unsure about the benefits of family sessions. It was more than likely that the father, and other family members too, had similar doubts. The story acknowledged these and made them something the therapist had shared in the past, and a natural response under the circumstances.

The therapist was surprised by the amount he learned in the family interview.   The story suggests that because the therapist was just learning about working with families, he was not expecting a lot from family interviews; hence his surprise when a lot happened. His feelings, as expressed in the story, probably corresponded to the father's. Before this conversation the father did not expect that a great deal would be achieved in a family interview, but the therapist, by mentioning his own surprise, helped open up to him the possibility that he might be surprised too.

The father was a very perceptive person, and during the family interview he contributed helpful information about the family. The father mentioned in the story is presented as a perceptive giver of information, not in any way as part of the problem or the cause of the daughter's difficulties. This should help the father attend therapy sessions, because it presents a less threatening and more realistic view of the process than the one he had before.

The therapist only appreciated certain things when he saw the whole family group. These things included the older daughters' closeness and the contrast between their appearance and that of the identified patient. Even though the mother had described the closeness of the two older girls, the full picture only became apparent to the therapist when he met everyone face-to-face.

The family described was "a basically healthy, normal" one. In other words problems such as those described can occur in "normal" families. This is perhaps the most contentious implied message; some might insist that for there to be problems as serious as Patricia's there must be something at least fairly seriously wrong with the family. But the fact is that terms like "normal" and "healthy," when applied to families, are vague. In most respects the family under consideration was normal. It is hardly statistically abnormal to have one teenage child who has acted out as Patricia had been doing. What *is* important in such cases is to help the family make whatever changes are needed to overcome their problems. Labeling them "abnormal," "disturbed," "dysfunctional" or anything else pejorative, does not help solve their problems and may even prevent them from getting into therapy. This applies even when a family's problems are far greater than those of Patricia's family or the family with whom this story was used.

Metaphors for use in these situations need not be taken from work with other families. An example of the use of another scenario is to be found in the anecdote that opens the introduction to this book. In that case the reluctant father was a foreman on a construction project. The metaphor used, which was addressed to the mother but intended primarily for the father, described how work on another construction project—a hospital (something the therapist, a physician, would know about)—failed to progress because the plumbers were on strike. The analogy between the father's role in the family and the plumber's role in the construction project was strikingly effective, in that the father's attitude changed almost immediately.

It is important to embed metaphorical messages in scenarios that are meaningful to the clients concerned. Had the father been a soldier, the absent person might have been the unit commander; if he had been a musician it might have been a key member of the orchestra, and so on.

Motivating Families to Become Involved in Therapy

This process often follows on from that of motivating families to get involved in assessment. Sometimes the same story can be continued. Thus the saga of Patricia's family could have been continued had problems arisen in keeping the family concerned in therapy.

In getting people involved in treatment therapists again have the option of telling stories—either apocryphal or true but disguised—about other clients or families or of picking metaphors from other areas of life. Erickson's (1980e) story of Joe (see Chapter 3) is useful in giving hope to the families of children with severe, chronic delinquency. The story suggests not only that change is possible in even the most severe and apparently hopeless case, but that it can occur quickly, even overnight, given the right combination of circumstances.

Reframing Behavioral Problems as Disorders of Socialization

When parents come for help for these children they often assume, understandably, that there is something wrong with the child. In a sense this is true, of course, but it can be helpful to reframe the problem as due to difficulties in the socialization process.

Reframing can often be accomplished quickly, easily, and neatly without the use of metaphor or any other indirect therapy device. As the parents, or perhaps the teacher or other adult who is complaining of the child's behavior, describes the child's misdeeds, the therapist can respond with remarks like, "So you are having trouble controlling Bill," or "It seems that up till now you haven't found a successful way of dealing with Claire's behavior," or "Nothing you've tried so far has worked, so I guess you're in need of a few new ideas."

All these responses carry the message that the problem will be solved when the parents find effective ways of dealing with the child, or at least with the child's problem behaviors. The problem is thus reframed as the parents' need to develop new strategies in their efforts to socialize their child, rather than as a disorder afflicting the child.

Unfortunately this simple device, even when used repeatedly —as it can be in one or a series of interviews—is not always effective. The parents may reject the idea that there is anything more they can possibly try; they may have had advice or suggestions from other therapists and found that when they tried to do as advised they failed; or they may have been to parent effectiveness courses, or other courses in which parenting skills are taught, only to find that what they learned "didn't work" with their children. In these circumstances the reframing has to be done indirectly, and metaphorical methods may be helpful.

The story at the start of this chapter is designed to reframe antisocial behavior as representing a need for different behavior control methods. Like most of the stories in this book it will require some modification to make its points correspond with the features of any family you are treating. There are obvious risks in comparing training dogs with training children, but if you take proper care in the presentation of the metaphor, you will find you can make such comparisons acceptable to the families you treat.

Sometimes the problem is not that the parents have failed to try appropriate methods of socializing their children, but that they haven't used these methods consistently and with conviction. Yet they may maintain that they have tried "everything." Metaphors can be helpful in persuading such parents that there is more to be considered than just whether they have tried each behavior control device. My colleague, Karen Rempel, has used the analogy of a glove. A glove has the same four fingers and thumb that a hand has; alone it can do nothing, but put a hand in it and it can do all kinds of things. Anecdotes such as the following can make similar points.

> One of the things I never understood when I was at school—and I still don't fully understand—was why some teachers could keep order and others couldn't, despite the fact that they seemed to use the same disciplinary methods.
> In my school there were only a few things the teachers could do if you misbehaved. They could make you write lines, award you a period of detention after classes were over, or report or send you to the school principal, who might give you a beating. Despite the use of these measures, some teachers failed to control their classes, which were often quite chaotic. Others, though, always had quiet and attentive classes, in which students seldom misbehaved; and most of these teachers made little use of the punishments available. They almost seemed to have some magic about them, but I think it was really their confident attitude and the fact that they *knew* they could control the class, that was important. Somehow we students also instinctively knew that these teachers just wouldn't tolerate any misbehavior.

* * *

> I sometimes see parents who are using sound behavior control methods, but nevertheless get into battles with their children. These are often children who have been getting their own way for a long time; when, at last, they find they're being treated in a firm and consistent way, with definite limits on the behaviors that are permitted, they're inclined to rebel, perhaps violently. They're not going to give up control that easily.

I've seen families in which this has taken the parents by surprise, and they've even thought their children were getting worse, not better. Actually it's a good sign. It means the parents have identified the real issues. It's a bit like soldiers advancing during a military campaign. When they start drawing the enemy's fire it means they're approaching something important.

I've noticed that battles are usually won by the side that has the most determination to win. It's figuring out ways of giving people determination that's the problem.

Parents who have difficulty becoming sufficiently confident, so that they can deal in a resolute way with their wayward children, can also often be helped through the use of the "self-esteem building" techniques described in Chapter 10.

Other Types of Reframing

Developmental reframing relabels "disturbed" behavior as "young" behavior—or possibly occasionally as behavior that is prematurely old. Stories about animals or children who were thought to be abnormal but turned out to be just behaving young for their years can be used as metaphors for this process. So can stories about machinery and products put into service before they are fully developed.

Antisocial behavior can also be reframed as serving one or several specific functions, such as establishing the limits of what is permissible, discovering what consequences follow particular actions, taking risks in order to liven up a dull life, or drawing attention away from other problems or tensions in a family. If metaphor is to be used to accomplish such reframing, the therapist again has the choice either of telling stories about other families or of using stories or anecdotes about other situations. These might be the animal world, the world of scientific research (I have used Sir Alexander Fleming's discovery of penicillin), the industrial world (in which waste products are sometimes found to have uses which at first were not apparent), or any other area with which the therapist is familiar.

Fleming's discovery of penicillin was serendipitous. He was working in his laboratory with some disease-causing bacteria. These were growing on a culture plate which became contaminated by a mold. Some investigators would probably have thrown the contaminated plate out, but Fleming took a look at it and noticed that the bacteria were dying where the mold was growing. This proved to be due to a substance produced by the mold, later named penicillin. So things should not always be taken at their face value. Similarly, if parents consider their children's behavior carefully they may discover unexpected things; for example their attention may be drawn to problems in their interaction as a parental couple.

Incidentally the term *serendipity* is derived from an interesting Persian fairy tale, *The Three Princes of Serendip*, which itself has some potential for use as a therapeutic metaphor. In this story the heroes possess the gift of making fortunate discoveries by accident.

Suggesting New Approaches and Possible Solutions

Therapists sometimes wish to suggest specific changes in the behavior or attitudes of children with behavior problems, or in the way parents respond to such behavior. For example, parents sometimes fall into the "negative reinforcer trap" (Wahler, 1976). This happens when they give attention to "negative," that is, undesired, behavior and ignore "positive," or desired, behavior. Thus when the child is behaving well the parents, figuratively speaking, heave a sigh of relief and get on with their other activities. They continue with these until the child next engages in some form of negative behavior. Then they give their attention once again to the child.

This pattern can often be changed for the better by explaining to the parents that they should alter their responses to reinforce the desired behavior and ignore, as far as possible, that which is not desired. The same point can be made by the use of anecdotes and stories. When dealing with parents who resist direct injunctions, tales can be told about children who —you really don't know how—got into a repetitive habit of obtaining attention by behaving badly; this led to things getting worse and worse as the parents responded to this behavior with attention and concern. Similar tales can be built around the behavior of domestic animals, the staff of commercial enterprises, children in school classes or other situations outside the home, or indeed any social situation with which the therapist is familiar.

SUMMARY

Antisocial behavior in children usually has multiple causes, but a frequent factor seems to be a failure in the process of social training. Although some children are harder to train than others and constitutional and other social factors play their parts in contributing to these problems, failure of the family's function in promoting the socialization process is often a key feature of these cases. In many cases it is also the easiest factor to remedy, for constitutionally determined temperamental factors are hard to modify, and the wider social environment is also usually difficult to alter.

The difficulty some families have in promoting satisfactory social behavior in their children is often but one aspect of generally poor family functioning. As a result, in most cases, treatment is best carried out with the family group, rather than being directed primarily to the individual who is displaying the antisocial behavior.

Metaphorical communication may be useful in motivating families to become involved in both assessment and treatment; in reframing antisocial behavior as a disorder of socialization; in presenting it as immature behavior; in reframing it as serving such purposes as exploring the permitted limits of behavior, discovering what consequences follow, or livening up a dull life; and in suggesting other previously unconsidered approaches or possible solutions. In families not open to the direct communication of such ideas, metaphorical approaches may prove successful.

A PRACTICAL EXERCISE

You are acting as a consultant to your local school board. A teacher and her principal consult you about a nine-year-old boy whose behavior in the classroom is causing great concern. Although his parents insist that he causes no difficulty at home, he has been a major disciplinary problem in the classroom since the start of the current school year five months previously. By talking constantly and being generally disobedient he takes up an inordinate amount of his teacher's time. He seems to enjoy the attention he gets as a result of his behavior, even though he has received a variety of punishments.

Develop a metaphor or metaphors that will help the teachers understand this boy's difficult behavior and offer them some ideas about how to deal with it.

7

Metaphors for
Emotional Problems

SOME ERICKSONIAN ANECDOTES

One of the highlights of the Second International Congress on Ericksonian Approaches to Hypnosis and Psychotherapy was a session in which six of Milton Erickson's children talked about their experiences of being brought up by this remarkable man. As they all recounted different anecdotes, one theme kept recurring.

One of the daughters, Betty Alice, described a trip she, her brother Robert, and their father took to Oak Creek Canyon in Arizona. The two children decided to move a lot of "huge boulders" around so as to form their initials. It was raining and cold, and the task was exhausting, but eventually they completed it. And when they rejoined their father they found that they could, if they knew exactly where to look with their binoculars, and if they looked *very* carefully, just make out the initials.

On the way home Betty Alice and her brother complained about how tired they were and about their sore muscles and skinned hands. They felt they had wasted their time and efforts for nothing—or at least just to have their initials where no one would ever see them. Their father's response was to tell them that when they looked back on this inci-

108

dent they would realize they had made a pretty wise investment. He predicted that when, in the years ahead, they
compared the amount of effort they had expended with the
number of smiles they had enjoyed whenever they remembered the incident, they would find he was right.

Betty Alice didn't accept this idea at the time. She thought,
"Well, that's just Daddy." But later she realized he was
right, for here she was, 30 years later, telling the tale with
evident delight.

The Erickson family moved around a fair amount and
lived in several different places. These all had their various
drawbacks but, as Betty Alice explained, their father always
emphasized the things they "liked best" about where they
lived. He took the same attitude about other things the family did: if you go to a cocktail party to please someone, or
out of a sense of duty, you decide to enjoy yourself. Presumably there has to be someone of interest there, or something
to be learned about some aspect of the human condition.
The event can perhaps be a challenge to you to discover
something interesting, revealing, enjoyable or in some way
worthwhile about an experience that on the surface may not
have much to recommend it.

Another anecdote was told by Robert. It concerned an incident his father used as one of his "teaching tales." When
Robert was about four he suffered a fall and split his lip. He
was bleeding profusely and in a lot of pain. Robert described
in some detail how his father dealt with this situation. He
first established communication with his son by acknowl-
edging that the injury hurt: "It hurts real bad," he said,
something Robert could easily identify with. Erickson then
put into words Robert's conviction that it was going to keep
on hurting and also his wish that it would stop hurting. But
then he added, "And maybe it will in a little while," thus
directing attention to the possible future cessation of the
pain.

Robert was then taken into the house so that his parents
and he (using a mirror) could examine the injury. His father
commented on the blood Robert had lost—"a lot of blood"—
and also on the fact that it was "good, strong, red blood"

which, when mixed with water, would turn pink. This indeed it did when the wound was washed with water.

The next step was the suturing of the wound. Because it was small, his father explained, Robert would not be able to have as many stitches as some of his siblings had had for some of their injuries; but on the other hand he would have more than some of the others had had on other occasions.

Then there was Kristina, the youngest of the Erickson children, who spoke of their father's use of "practice." When things presented difficulty for the Erickson children, for example putting away the Monopoly set when the game was over, or making their beds, he would make them spend appropriate periods of time—even as long as two hours—practicing these activities. It wasn't a punishment, of course, just the practicing of a useful skill!

REFRAMING AND THE TREATMENT OF EMOTIONAL DISORDERS

What have these stories to do with emotional disorders and their treatment? Each of the incidents described has two particular characteristics: it involves *a reframing of an experience*, and it offers *a view of an incident from a later point in time*. These two processes—reframing and considering how things appear when looked back upon later—can help clients deal with certain kinds of emotional problems. I have used all of the stories just recounted in the course of therapy with individuals or families, though never all in the same session.

EMOTIONAL DISORDERS

Emotional disorders are a big and mixed group. The third edition of the American Psychiatric Association's *Diagnostic and Statistical Manual*, the *DSM-III* (American Psychiatric Association, 1980), lists and defines the following disorders, each one of which is characterized by some form of disturbance of the emotional state of affected individuals: "affective disorders," "anxiety disorders," "somatoform disorders," "conversion disorders," and "dissociative (or hysterical) disorders." Each of these is subdivided, though the subcategories need not concern us here, and each involves a disorder of mood; this may be in the direction of excessive anxiety, or it may take the form of depression or elation. Anxiety may be expressed directly or—through the operation of mental defense mechanisms—indirectly in such symptoms as obsessions, compulsions, phobias, conversion symptoms, or dissociative phenomena. However anxiety or other emotional difficulties (for example, depression) are expressed, there is usually a need for some psychotherapeutic help. In the course of providing this, therapeutic metaphors can sometimes be very useful.*

While therapeutic metaphors are no panacea for emotional and other psychiatric problems, they can be useful adjuncts in the psychotherapy of the anxious, the unhappy, the depressed and the grieving. People's worries, fears, and feelings of failure can sometimes be reframed and seen differently. Do so directly often fails, just as telling the depressed person to "cheer up" does, but reframing a situation metaphorically may be successful.

METAPHORICAL REFRAMING

How may stories such as those set out at the start of this chapter assist in the treatment of emotional problems? Each story has several possible meanings, and what a person gets from it will depend not only on its content but on the person's psychological state and on how the story is told. We will look first at some of the messages contained in each story; then we will consider how they may be applied clinically. The number of meanings any story may have is very great, perhaps infinite, depend-

---

*Careful assessment must, of course, always precede the treatment of any psychiatric disorder. Biological factors apppear to play an important part in the etiology of some of the conditions referred to here, notably the major affective disorders; in these cases pharmacological treatment, perhaps with antidepressant drugs or lithium carbonate, may be indicated. In other cases, where psychological causative factors predominate, psychotherapy is often the main treatment modality and therapeutic metaphor may be useful.

ing on the experiences, attitudes, state of mind, personality, and knowledge of the hearer. In the summary that follows, therefore, we shall consider only some of the more obvious themes contained in these particular tales.

The story about the rocks made to form initials. The subjects' experience was at first seemingly futile. They worked hard in wet and cold weather and got sore hands and muscles. At the end of it all their initials could hardly be seen, and no one who did not know where to look (and who would?) was going to see their handiwork. They felt they had wasted their time. But then they were offered a different way of viewing their experience. When they looked back at it in the future, they were told, it would seem like a wise investment of their time and energy. One child at least rejected this idea at the time. Yet it was not forgotten, and in the fullness of time what their father had said proved correct.

This story does not just suggest that things may look different from a future perspective. It also suggests that our life experiences can have different sorts of values. The children felt that what they had done was futile because no one would ever see and appreciate the result. But the concrete results of our activities are not always important; sometimes it is the cooperative activity that achieves the result that is of most value. Indeed, how many of our activities leave any tangible result at all? And why did Betty Alice and Robert gain so much pleasure from the memory of this experience? Presumably because they were enjoying themselves at the time; the memory of working together to move the rocks into the desired positions evoked memories also of the enjoyment they had experienced at the time. To use the terminology of neurolinguistic programming, the two experiences—working and enjoying—had become "anchored" to each other.

Also significant in the story is the identity of the person who offered the different view of what the children had done. This person is both the children's father and a world-famous psychotherapist. Either or both identities might have special meaning for clients. A therapist would probably not want to use the story in the present form with clients whose attitudes towards their fathers were hostile and rebellious—unless the purpose was to elicit a paradoxical response. But in some clinical situations attributing the reframed view of the situation to someone with status, like a famous psychotherapist, might give it added weight. If that were considered an important part of the therapeutic plan it would probably be wise to include in the story rather more information about Erickson as a skilled, innovative, and generally remarkable therapist, than appears in the foregoing account.

If a client rejects the reframed view of the situation that is being offered, despite the buildup that Erickson (or any other authority who might be used in the metaphor) has been given, it is still not the therapist's opinion that the client is questioning but that of a third party. Again we have the advantage that therapist and client do not confront each other in an adversarial way. And these stories can be introduced in an almost casual way; for example, "We've a few minutes left—I wonder if you'd be interested in a story I heard at a conference I attended recently (or last year or whenever it was)?"

The account of the family's frequent moves. When the Erickson children were growing up the family moved several times and, we are told, some of the places where they lived had their drawbacks. And what place does not have at least some drawbacks? The story makes the simple point that we can always choose between looking at the positive aspects of a situation or the negative ones. There may be advantages, it suggests, in giving our main attention to what is positive.

The story of the split lip. This tale is rich in meaning. It starts with a description of how Erickson established rapport with his injured son; he accepted the way his son felt—the pain, the fear that the pain would continue for a long time, the wish that it would stop. When faced with people in distress, the story says, accept the way they feel without argument.

But once he is in a state of rapport with his son, Erickson begins to reframe things. There are some good things about this otherwise unfortunate situation. The blood is "good, strong blood," a healthy sign. When mixed with water it goes pink, as it should. Robert is experiencing something his siblings have already gone through; he is made to feel one with them when the number of stitches he is to receive is compared with the numbers they received for their injuries. And by referring to injuries that Robert's siblings have suffered, Erickson perhaps puts the incident into context as one of the things that are part of life. But how much better to do it this way than by saying, "There, there, these things happen, you must be brave!"

Practicing things one has not done properly. Finally we come to Kristina Erickson's account of how her father made the children "practice" carrying out household and other tasks that they had failed to perform properly, on time, or at all. Some might call this punishment, but Erickson chose to call it practice. It is thus another example of reframing: things can have different meanings and values. They can be looked at in different ways. By analogy, therefore, adverse experiences generally can be of benefit to us; almost any burdensome time in a person's life may have value as a learning experience. In facing and dealing with things that present us with difficulty, we are obtaining practice in dealing with such situations; everything we do well, even if we do not like doing it, is good practice and we can learn from it. (In another story told by one of the children, Erickson was described as making even sweeping the floor of the basement kitchen enjoyable!)

CLINICAL APPLICATIONS

People suffering from emotional distress are usually reacting to some form of environmental stress. The stress may be great or small, and the individual's reaction may or may not seem excessive when judged against the apparent severity of the stress. Nevertheless, reframing the situation, or certain aspects of it, may be helpful.

An example of reframing in a therapeutic setting is afforded by a family who came to psychiatric attention because of the "seizures" of Rick, the 10-year-old son. Rick lived at home with his parents, Arthur and Betty, married 20 years, and his brothers Tom (17) and Stuart (13). An older sister, Ursula (19), was living in an apartment in another part of the city and had a job working as a secretary–receptionist for a physician. Another daughter, Vivienne, had been killed when the truck in which she was traveling, with her 6-month-old baby and her boy friend, the father of the baby, hit a tanker truck head on at high speed. This had happened two years previously when Vivienne was 16, but long before that she had been a source of concern to her parents. After several years of behavioral problems, she had left home and dropped out of school at 15 and then became pregnant. Tom, too, had left home a year previously, but he returned a few weeks before the first interview with the family. Stuart's behavior at home was satisfactory, but at school he was said to have both behavioral and academic problems.

Rick had been diagnosed as having epilepsy two years previously, although his electroencephalogram had never been abnormal. He was given anticonvulsant medication, and his seizures were described as well controlled until about two months previously. Increasingly frequent and bizarre "seizures" then appeared. Rick would have up to 30 attacks per day, and concern about the escalation of symptoms greatly preoccupied his mother, who gave up her part-time job to be at home with her youngest son.

When the family was seen an overwhelming aura of sadness was evident. It seemed that no one had adequately mourned, or come to terms with, the deaths of Vivienne and her baby and boyfriend. The parents spoke of how the accident occurred just as they were making friends with their daughter again, after a period during which they had been estranged. They felt she was on the way to getting her life together, and they had had great hopes for her and for their granddaughter. But now these hopes would never be realized.

Betty appeared depressed and wept during much of the interview. Arthur, while obviously sad, seemed to have largely withdrawn from the family's life and was burying himself in his business. Rick's seizures kept him at home where he could comfort his mother and where she could look after him. In the interview situation, Stuart was the least obviously upset, but it was noted that his school performance had started to fall off after Vivienne's death. Tom had followed Vivienne in dropping out of school and had been drifting aimlessly for the last year. Although now back in the household, he had no job, and Betty complained that he regularly came in drunk and created a disturbance in the family. Ursula was invited to the second family session, but declined to attend, saying that she did not wish to talk about the death of her sister, having heard that this was talked about in the first session.

It was clear that there were many problems in this family and that many had existed before Vivienne's death. Since that event, though, they had got worse and the family seemed to have become paralyzed so far as making any changes in their way of thinking or functioning was concerned. The enormity of their loss, and the guilt the parents felt about what had happened to Vivienne (whom they had told to leave the household when she became pregnant), still overwhelmed them. They seemed in a state of total despair.

Although many issues needed to be addressed in the family the foremost one, which overshadowed all else, was their sadness. Until their collective depression was ameliorated and they could be helped to come to terms with the loss of Vivienne, attempts to address other issues in therapy seemed futile. Many people had tried to help this family, both professionals and lay people, without much apparent success. At the conscious level Arthur and Betty, whose grief seemed central to the family's problems, knew that Vivienne and her son were gone and could never come back; they said too that they knew they had to get on with life without their dead daughter and granddaughter. They had spent hours and hours talking about Vivienne, how they had failed her, what they might have done better, how they felt now, and so on.

Therapeutic progress seemed to depend on altering the family's, and especially the parents', perception of past events, or at least directing their attention to different aspects of them. Perhaps they should dwell more on their good times with Vivienne, upon her virtues and strengths, on what they had learned from the harrowing experiences they had been through and on their hopes, plans, and prospects for the future. But how to get them to look at things differently?

Direct approaches to reframing the family's situation did not prove effective. The family members accepted, intellectually, what they were told, but continued unchanged as far as their emotional state was concerned. An attempt was therefore made to offer them some new ways of viewing their situation by the use of metaphor. They were first told, almost as an aside at the end of a session, about Milton Erickson and how he was so often able to find different ways of looking at things. The International Congress session at which his children spoke was mentioned, and the story of the boulders made to form initials was told them, with some elaboration of the points that things can always be looked at in various different ways, and that they often look different once one has the advantage of hindsight. There was a noticeable lightening of the family's mood when they were being told the story and, following that, when the therapist spoke about Erickson's sometimes surprising capacity to find unexpected and positive features in unlikely situations. The lightening of the family's mood, however, was quite brief.

One of the difficulties in psychotherapy is that of assessing the effect a given intervention has. It is probably unrealistic to expect any intervention in a family such as we are considering to bring about an immediate, dramatic change. The therapist might hope, rather, that an intervention would give rise to some unconscious—and perhaps conscious—reevaluation of the situation that might, in due course, lead to attitudinal and emotional changes. Whether these initial metaphors had helped Rick's family was hard to assess. In any event, more input of some sort was evidently needed.

Most therapists deciding to use metaphors in the course of treatment will sometimes want to use material from their own experience or imagination. The therapist who was treating this family next offered an experience from his own life.

When I left high school in England in 1948 the United Kingdom had compulsory national service—that is, service in one of the armed forces. Those who were going to study medicine, however, could be exempted from being called up for their two years' service until after they had qualified and completed their internship year. I opted to delay my call-up, so that in due course I served for two years as a medical officer in the British army. Most of my time was spent in Cyprus, which was then a British colony, though subject to terrorist activities by EOKA, a group that was demanding union with Greece.

My period of service in the army was interesting but also difficult. The national service medical officers got—at least we certainly believed we got—a bad deal. We were paid less than the regular officers, those who had signed on voluntarily, and got all the worst duties and postings. If someone had to be sent to an artillery regiment engaged in firing practice, to hang around in the rain and mud while the guns roared away day after day and nobody got injured, it would be one of us. It was we who were sent up into the mountains at a moment's notice to cover an army unit fighting the terrorists. We got the worst accommodations, usually in tents, and we were allocated the least desirable duty hours. In short, we were generally at the bottom of the medical totem pole.

At the time I didn't think I was enjoying my spell in the army and to this day there's no doubt in my mind that I was sometimes very unhappy. At other times I was just bored, but nearly always I felt that my medical career was getting nowhere. And yet when I look back now on those days I no longer feel the unhappiness; instead I think of some fine people I met and got to know and I recall the beauty of the island of Cyprus. I realize that I learned a lot of things about life and its frustrations and rewards and I observed human behavior in settings quite different from any I had experienced before or have since.

I sometimes wish I'd been able at the time to realize what I was learning, and to see that there were many more positive things going on for me than I thought. Actually one of my fellow officers did many times assure me that if I could cope with the army I could cope with anything. An exaggeration, no doubt, but he had a point, I'd say, looking back.

This story seemed to have some impact on the family, but of course therapy required much more than just a reframing of the death of Vivienne and related issues. The family continued in therapy for many months, and a number of other therapeutic devices were employed, in addition to the use of metaphor.

An issue that is liable to arise when the use of metaphor is being considered is that of how much self-disclosure by the therapist is appropriate. Although the use by therapists of their own personal experiences can add power to their interventions, many therapists, quite naturally, do not wish to share details of their personal lives with their clients. As a general rule, moreover, they should not do so; to involve their clients in their own lives would be a major therapeutic error. At the same time, however, many believe that there are times when it is helpful to make an exception to this rule, and the therapist made one in working with this family.

The experience he shared was the death, from a cerebral tumor, of his 8-year-old daughter some 16 years previously. He was able to tell the family that he could identify with many of their feelings of outrage and loss. He could tell them that his daughter's death had had extensive repercussions, which continued for a few years, in his family. He was also able to say that now, when his wife and he looked back on this time, much of the sadness had gone, and they could even begin to feel glad they had their daughter for as long as they did. They also realized that they had learned things of value from their unhappy experience. One of these was a better understanding of bereavement and of how to talk to people who have suffered the loss of a loved one. "And of course," the therapist said, "I'm able to share this with you now." His experience thus became a metaphor for theirs.

All therapists have in their own histories experiences that can be of value to their clients. Occasionally they may be able to use them in their therapy practice. This should be used done sparingly, however, and only after careful consideration. Moreover it is possible, and sometimes best, to tell your story as if it were someone else's, starting with, "I knew a therapist who . . . " or "I heard a story the other day about . . . "

In the case of Rick's family, the therapist's act of self-disclosure seemed to be of real help. The family slowly adjusted to their losses and made progress in mourning their daughter's death and that of her baby. Gradually, they turned to deal constructively with their other problems.

METAPHORS FOR OTHER EMOTIONAL PROBLEMS

Metaphors can be devised for most, perhaps all, ideas and concepts that therapists wish to convey to their unhappy, anxious, grieving, or depressed patients. The principles of metaphor construction set out in Chapter 3 should be used in constructing metaphors. Sometimes metaphorical tasks can be used when an impasse has been reached in therapy, as in the case of Phoebe.

A Metaphorical Ritual

Phoebe, 11 years old, had parents who were both professional people and a 15-year-old brother, Martin, who was doing well at school and was not thought to have any problems. The previous summer Phoebe had started to show some concerns about the signs of puberty she was developing; she became reluctant to wear clothes that revealed her early breast development and she would not wear skirts or dresses, only pants.

In September Phoebe was placed in an "enriched" program at school. A month or two later she started to worry unduly about her progress, which actually was quite satisfactory. In November her school class visited a hospital for the chronically ill, and she saw an old man vomit. After this Phoebe became anxious that she might vomit, and she developed a number of rituals that, she told her parents, would prevent her from vomiting. (She never actually did vomit throughout the whole course of events.)

Eventually Phoebe was admitted to hospital because of loss of weight and with a diagnosis of anorexia nervosa. This diagnosis proved incorrect; she had been losing weight only because her mealtime rituals prevented her eating much during the limited time which, on professional advice, the parents had permitted her for her meals. It became clear that she was suffering from an obsessive–compulsive disorder and she was transferred to the psychiatric unit.

Phoebe proved a difficult patient to treat. At first her symptoms got steadily worse, until she was largely crippled by her obsessional thoughts and rituals. Dressing, eating a meal, even walking across the room, became major undertakings, so complex were the rituals involved. She was quite resistant to psychotherapy and to various other treatment methods, including response prevention (according to some—e.g., Stanley, 1980—the most effective method of treating ritualistic behavior), and all of these proved ineffective. Phoebe was then given the following task.

In the hospital school, which Phoebe attended daily, every time she was observed to be engaging in any sort of ritual, she was required to run round the gymnasium twice or, as an alternative at the teacher's discretion, to undertake some other form of exercise, such as a prescribed number of push-ups.

Phoebe was by nature a conscientious, compliant, and obsessional girl. Noncompliance became a problem only when the strength of her obsessive–compulsive drives made it impossible for her to do as she was told. It was probably because of these characteristics that she performed the ritual prescribed for her with little or no protest. The results were dramatic. Phoebe's symptoms rapidly subsided. The program was soon extended to the inpatient unit itself and then to the home, where the family implemented it during weekend passes from the hospital. It soon became routine for all concerned with Phoebe to tell her to exercise as soon as she was observed carrying out any ritual. This promptly put a stop to the ritualistic behavior.

Phoebe was soon discharged from hospital and, as this is written, has been followed up for over two years. The exercise program has been presented to her and her family as lifelong; if she were to show any ritualistic behavior at any time she should be told to exercise, though it is a long while since she has had to do so.

Why did this unconventional treatment for a severe obsessive–compulsive disorder work? It has some, but not all, of the features of "ordeal therapy," as described by Haley (1984). Haley, developing a procedure originated by Erickson, describes a series of clients who had proved resistant to other treatments and who were then challenged to undertake an ordeal, the nature of which they were not told until after they had agreed to perform it. They were guaranteed, however, that the treatment would work if they carried it out. The ordeal was something that was harmless in itself, or even beneficial, but worse for the client than the symptom. The client has to perform the ritual if the symptom persists; for example, an insomniac man had to spend the night waxing and polishing the kitchen floor if he didn't sleep. He soon found it more pleasant to go to sleep!

Phoebe had an ordeal to perform, but it was not presented to her as Haley presented his clients with their ordeals. Instead we relied on Phoebe's obsessional characteristics to ensure that she carried out the task set her.

Rather than regard this as an example of ordeal therapy, it may be more accurate to look upon the exercise ritual as a metaphor for the compulsive rituals Phoebe had been engaging in. One set of rituals—various forms of exercise—had been substituted for the others. Whatever the unconscious meaning of her symptoms may have been—and this never became entirely clear, though there was a fear of vomiting and of growing up—the prescribed rituals served as metaphors for the original compulsive rituals and presumably took on the functions of those rituals. Much secondary gain had resulted from the original symptoms; before admission Phoebe had become the center of the family's life and the object of much concern and solicitude. Being told to exercise, though, did not provide much secondary gain; she didn't particularly enjoy it, even though she was told it was good for her, and it was prescribed in a matter-of-fact way, without any special attention being given her.

Brad the Brat

Tom was a serious-looking bespectacled boy of 11 years. He was an excellent student and a keen athlete; he was especially good at hockey and football. For about a year before he came to hospital, however, he had had recurrent and compulsive urges to plunge his fingers, or other objects such as spoons or pencils, down his throat, inducing vomiting. These episodes had got more frequent, intense, and alarming for Tom and his parents over the last year.

Tom's urges did not seem to be based on any suicidal wishes, but were rather felt by him to be irrational, absurd, and involuntary. His parents had noticed him becoming increasingly unhappy and depressed, easily prone to tears and babyish whenever he experienced stress, and to him the slightest imperfection in his school work, real or imagined, was a serious stress.

In his first therapy session Tom spoke cheerfully and confidently, especially about sports. When asked about his "problem," however, a swift and dramatic change occurred. His voice became high-pitched and whining, and he cried copiously as he described his irrational urges. The therapist asked him what he would like to do to overcome this urge, and quickly he said he would like to tell it to go away. The therapist agreed with this suggested solution and asked Tom if he had ever been able to do this with anyone or anything he didn't like.

Tom reflected, then brightened up; he related an encounter in the school yard with a boy called Brad. Brad was a big, burly boy, known to be a bully. Tom's chest rose as he recalled the momentous day when he had mustered the necessary courage to challenge Brad and defeat him. He called Brad a brat. The therapist then asked him if his "uncontrollable" urges were somewhat like "Brad the Brat." At this Tom beamed. He agreed that "Brad the Brat" was the perfect name for them.

With guidance from the therapist, Tom was able to retrace all his experiences of choking himself, but this time he reexperienced them completely differently, superimposing the image of Brad the Brat on them and at the same time recalling the feelings of mastery and confidence he associated with his conflict with Brad. He left the office looking cheerful and in a buoyant mood; his compulsive symptoms never recurred.

Despite the resolution of Tom's compulsive urges, he remained subject to overwhelming anxiety in the classroom. The following story was therefore composed for him.

> Jenny was a little girl with great musical talent. She dreamed of being one of the world's great violinists and of playing in the finest orchestras under famous conductors. Her mother had selected for her the best teacher in their city, and Jenny worked hard.
>
> Eventually the teacher decided that the time had come for Jenny to give a recital. Jenny worked harder than ever before to prepare for it but, to her dismay, she found she was playing less and less well, rather than better. Her teacher told her to work even harder, but things only got worse. Then her teacher had an amazing thought: perhaps Jenny was working too hard, and instead of practicing more, maybe she should practice less!
>
> Jenny was most surprised when her teacher told her to practice less. How could that help her do well in the recital? But she did as she was told and, much to her surprise, but also her delight, she felt calmer and more relaxed, and she played better. She was again able to produce sweet and beautiful sounds on her beloved instrument. And she played magnificently in her recital.

This summary of some of the work done during therapy with Tom illustrates the use of two metaphorical devices. In the first, "Brad the Brat" became a metaphor for the resources Tom had within him to overcome his problem. The actual therapy process was really an example of respondent conditioning, although the situations were experienced in fantasy only. Tom was invited to imagine each of the situations in which he experienced his irrational urge, but his feelings of confidence and competence in defeating Brad were now paired with this urge, which was therefore defeated also.

The second metaphor was presented as a simple anecdote to which Tom listened carefully; he responded to it by moderating his formerly rather frantic, obsessive efforts to perform superlatively at school. His anxiety level fell, although other therapeutic measures, including discussion with Tom's teachers about how his anxious behavior should be handled, were also employed.

METAPHORS FOR DEPRESSED PEOPLE

Depression is one of the most prevalent emotional disorders. Metaphors can play a useful part in the treatment of some depressed people. Here again the first step to be taken, before any treatment is started, is to carry out a thorough assessment of the patient and to decide whether treatment should be psychotherapeutic, psychopharmacological, or sociological. In many cases more than one of these approaches may be indicated.

Many different psychotherapy approaches may be needed in dealing with depressed individuals. When metaphors are to be used they must be individually constructed to meet the needs of the case, using the principles set out in Chapter 3. One almost universal requirement, however, is to assure depressed clients that they will get better, that things will look brighter in the future, even if there seems no hope of this at the moment. Stories may be told about long, weary journeys which seem to be unending and lead those undertaking them to feel a profound sense of despair, but which unexpectedly end in something exciting, beautiful, or in some way rewarding.

One such story might be that of a journey through the Sinai desert, a most depressing place, and up the Jordan valley that ends, dramatically and unexpectedly, with a view of the magnificent, lush oasis of Jericho. This metaphor might be particularly meaningful to clients who have studied the Old Testament and are aware of how dispirited the Israelites became during their years in the wilderness, before they finally saw the promised land.

For others a metaphor from the contemporary business world might be better. An example is afforded by the long, hard, and frequently disappointing work of drilling for oil and natural gas in Canada's Beaufort Sea. For years a number of oil companies braved the bitter Arctic conditions, with all the expense and problems involved, with little return. The leaders of these companies began to think that all their efforts and the billions of dollars they had spent had been wasted; they became quite depressed and almost gave up. Then in September 1984, after many false hopes had been dashed, Gulf Oil Resources Inc., of Calgary, reported on the drilling results from the Amauligak J-44 well. This had a calculated production capacity of 13,600 barrels of oil per day, a most encouraging result and one that made the situation in the Beaufort Sea look quite different and much more promising.

We therapists have all had our times of despondency—even of despair—times that have ended in a happy event or other outcome. These too, perhaps modified to suit the needs of the particular people we are treating, may be developed into metaphors that can assist our depressed clients.

SUMMARY

The use of metaphors may contribute to the treatment of clients with emotional disorders by reframing their situations in different, and usually more hopeful, terms. Severely anxious individuals and, even more so, those who are depressed, often have difficulty seeing the positive side of things; when a direct approach to dealing with such issues fails, the therapist may suggest a different view of the situation by the use of one or more of the various metaphorical methods described in earlier chapters.

The fact that adverse experiences can be of benefit to us is often hard to accept. Metaphors can sometimes be more effective in putting over the message that we can learn useful new skills as we overcome our problems. Such points are particularly difficult for those who are depressed or very worried to accept; such people are often better able to accept metaphorical input than direct explanations.

Metaphors can be helpful in enabling people to obtain access to the resources they need to overcome anxiety and anxiety-related symptoms.

In treating depressed people, an important part of the therapist's task is to instill hope. Telling clients that they will get better and that things will not always look as black as they do currently may not be successful. In such instances, stories about sudden or unexpected changes occurring in people's situations may help; emphasis on the surprise experienced when this happened may be useful when, as is often the case, clients are convinced things will not improve for them.

A PRACTICAL EXERCISE

Lionel, 46 years old, was formerly an executive with a large paper-making company but lost his job two months ago. He is still living on his severance pay, but is starting to look forward with apprehension to the day when it will run out. So far, all Lionel's efforts to find other employment have been unsuccessful.

This is Lionel's first experience of unemployment, and he is becoming increasingly anxious and depressed about his situation, not least because he has three school-age children to support and because his wife is also unemployed. He can see no way out of his present dilemma.

Devise a metaphorical approach that might help Lionel look at his situation differently and that might also assist him in taking a constructive approach to the problems he faces.

8

Metaphors for Family Problems

A TRUE STORY FROM THE WORLD OF JAZZ

The late Fletcher Henderson was a talented jazz musician, arranger, and composer. His career as a bandleader got off to an auspicious start in the 1920s, when he led one of the first of the larger jazz bands that were then emerging. Such notable musicians as Louis Armstrong, Coleman Hawkins, Don Redman, Tommy Ladnier and Buster Bailey played in his band. But although he employed some of the finest musicians of the day, Henderson was in some respects a poor bandleader. Lawrence Lucie, who for a time played guitar in Henderson's band, later spoke of his time with the band:

"A lot of times, when a guy came on late or some of the fellows didn't behave well, he could have been really angry and made them uncomfortable. Although he didn't like it, he didn't let them know it. But the others in the band would be mad with this guy who came late, because it could jeopardize the job. Everybody's ready and waiting up front, wanting to get together, and there's a big crowd, and here's this fellow coming late! Fletcher would put up with all that, and keep smiling, until we were ready and he could say, 'Okay!' Five minutes later he would be telling that same guy to take a solo, and not long after that he would be admiring what he played. So he had become a part of the whole thing, not like a leader, but like one of the band'' (Dance, 1974, p. 151–152).

Fletcher Henderson's band was ultimately a commercial failure. Even musically it did not live up to its earlier promise. Its record contrasts, for example, with those of the big bands of Duke Ellington, Count Basie, and Benny Goodman, which were well-led and efficiently functioning organizations. Indeed, Henderson eventually turned to writing and arranging for the Goodman orchestra.

Although in the quotation above Lawrence Lucie is praising Henderson, and talking about what a fine, relaxed leader he was, he also—unwittingly, no doubt—reveals what was probably the band's, or perhaps Henderson's, fatal flaw. This was a lack of firm leadership and a *laissez-faire* attitude on the part of the leader. Fletcher was an ''indulgent parent,'' too sweet and kind to his men, even though his guitarist, at least, was left with fond memories of his time in the band. The last sentence of the quotation makes it clear that Henderson was ''one of the boys,'' not their leader; there was no boundary between him and his musicians.

METAPHORS AND DYSFUNCTIONAL FAMILIES

The use of metaphors is but one of a number of strategic devices therapists may use to promote change in families. Any of the metaphorical devices discussed in Chapter 3 may be employed, but probably the easiest to use with family groups are stories. The functioning of a band is in some ways analogous to that of a family, hence the story above. Jazz bands may be particularly suitable, for reasons that will be mentioned later in the chapter.

The construction of metaphors for family problems is usually a more complex task than devising metaphors for use with individual clients, or even with couples. When stories are used to address family situations in a comprehensive way, devising characters and patterns of relationships that are isomorphic with actual family situations requires careful thought and planning. Particularly taxing may be the development in a metaphor of a sequence of events that is equivalent to the sequence of events in the life of an actual family.

Full-length stories addressing total family situations are not always the best metaphorical devices to use. Their complexity makes them often hard to construct, and their length requires good powers of concentration on the part of the families to whom they are offered. It is therefore often best to start by tackling specific aspects of family function. As therapy progresses metaphors can sometimes be extended, becoming more complex and comprehensive, so that eventually they have addressed all the issues with which therapy needs to deal. This chapter will take certain common examples of family dysfunction and consider how metaphorical devices may be used to help restore healthier and more adaptive functioning. The procedures discussed are intended for use as parts of wider treatment plans.

Metaphors generally need to be constructed specifically for the clients to whom they are to be offered, particularly in the case of families, which invariably have their own unique characteristics and ways of functioning. It is not possible, therefore, simply to have ready a stock of stories and to produce one or more of them when required. Even so, certain patterns do occur commonly in dysfunctional families, and to deal with these, it can be useful to have ready outlines within which to build up suitable stories or construct other types of metaphor. This chapter will offer some ideas and outline some story types that may assist therapists in constructing their own metaphors.

The family situations considered in this chapter are enmeshment, disengagement, the scapegoating of family members, problems of role assignment and performance, role confusion, and disturbed communication. These common types of family dysfunction are recognized by most family therapists, even though they may call them by different names. The reader should note, too, that the problems of family development we considered in Chapter 5 and the patterns of family dysfunction we are considering in this chapter are not mutually exclusive—far from it.

Terms such as *enmeshment* and *scapegoating* do not describe distinct clinical entities but, rather, represent shorthand descriptions of particular aspects of family structure (Minuchin, 1974) or functioning (Epstein et al., 1978), that are often observed in families seeking therapy. Terms like these, like all labels, run the risk of oversimplifying complex patterns of interactions and relationships. We will try to use these terms simply as convenient tag-names for some common phenomena occurring in dysfunctional family systems—some patterns of behavior that may be altered through the use of metaphor. Dysfunctional family patterns are myriad, and we can consider only a few in this chapter. The examples discussed, however, may give the therapist who works with families ideas that are applicable to many other clinical problems.

METAPHORS FOR FAMILY SITUATIONS

Before considering how metaphor may help restore more adaptive functioning in families, we will examine some of the infinite number of scenarios that can be used to address family problems metaphorically. Virtually any situation in which a group of people, animals, or fantasy figures of any sort is engaged in a collective endeavor may be used; within the group there should be different individuals, or groups of individuals, with various roles and responsibilities.

Which context to select for a particular family is probably less important than the care and skill devoted to the construction of the metaphor. Nevertheless, it is helpful to have a context that is as isomorphic as possible; in addition those of you who are just starting to explore the use of therapeutic metaphors may find it helpful to be offered examples, as an inspiration to develop your own.

The kinds of stories or metaphorical scenarios that you will be most comfortable using will depend in part on your own particular interests and knowledge; most of us feel more at ease talking about things of which we have at least some knowledge, rather than about those with which we are unfamiliar. In this connection, although choosing a context for the metaphor that is meaningful to the family (like the story told to a construction company foreman about problems on a construction site) can be helpful, there can be advantages in telling clients about things of which they know little or nothing. In such situations the therapist has to explain how the institution, group, or whatever is being used to contain the metaphorical meaning, operates, and therapeutic input can often be incorporated into such explanations.

Most human organizations are made up of individuals with differing roles; in general, they have leaders and are organized hierarchically. Without leadership and a suitable hierarchical structure, institutions, sports teams, industrial enterprises, school classes, and other organizations usually fail to function well. The importance attached to the role of leaders is demonstrated by the tendency of companies to fire managers, and for baseball, football and other teams to replace their coaches, when things go wrong. Similarly, people elect new governments when they feel they are not getting the right sort of leadership from those in office. Any of these examples, and many more, may be used in the construction of metaphors designed, for example, to illustrate the importance of good leadership. The importance of there being a clear boundary between those being led (like the members of a band, or the children in a family; and those doing the leading, that is the bandleader or the parents) may be pointed out metaphorically; the point can be made, too, that if there is confusion of roles the system—band, family or whatever it may be—is likely to function less well than otherwise it would.

Let us now consider the functioning of a jazz band, which can serve as a metaphor for some aspects of family functioning. Jazz, an improvised music, depends for its quality and success on the constructive and creative interplay of different musicians, playing a variety of instruments. A jazz band has its different parts; there is usually at least a "rhythm section" and a "front line." These have distinct functions. The rhythm section lays down the beat of the music. The front line instruments are responsible for the melodic lines and their interplay. The front line may be further divided into different instruments or groups of instruments, for example brass instruments and reed instruments; the players of each must know what they are supposed to be doing, and how what they are doing is distinct from but at the same time fits in with, what the other musicians are doing. The collective effort of the band as a whole also needs direction.

As you watch a jazz band playing you will see that the leader is continually giving instructions to the members of the band, setting the tempo for each tune; indicating when the musicians should take solos, and how long each should be; defining "riffs," which are repetitive musical patterns that the other musicians may play behind a soloist or at some other point during the performance of a piece; and of course letting the members of the band know when each tune should come to an end. Such instructions are often given quite unobtrusively, perhaps by a nod of the head, some other nonverbal cue or the use of a musical phrase or emphasis with which the musicians are familiar.

Sometimes the musicians have played together for so long that instructions are no longer needed. They know how their leader likes a certain tune played, who should take solos when, and so forth. Nevertheless, the leaders' decisions and authority are still in operation, even though the band is functioning so well and is so experienced and well-rehearsed, that few or no instructions need be given while they are playing. Some bands have dual leadership; this can work well, but it carries with it the risk of friction between the leaders.

Few, if any, therapeutic metaphors perfectly represent the clinical situations for which they are constructed, but there is a considerable resemblance between some aspects of the subsystems of a family and those of a jazz band. The metaphor of the functioning of a symphony orchestra could of course be used, as could many other forms of organization. A symphony orchestra has the same need for the smooth interaction of its different sections, each of which has specific functions distinct from those of the other sections, and also the same need for leadership. But it probably provides a less exact metaphor for a family than a jazz band does; for one thing it plays predetermined, composed pieces, rather than creating its own musical structure as it goes along. Few families are as ordered and predictable as a symphony orchestra.

Playing in a jazz band is predictable only up to a point; things are changing all the time, as the individual musicians, operating within the overall framework of the group, define their own melody lines and create their own mini-compositions while they play. Also when the members of a band stay together over a period of years, they develop new skills, learn new musical tricks and techniques, and extend their repertoire. In the same way the behaviors, and the emotional and physical states, of the members of a family are, typically, changing all the time. Thus constant adjustments must be made by each individual in the family, rather as jazz musicians adjust their playing according to what the other members of the group are doing.

The families we see are all faced with the task of making progress through the developmental stages discussed in Chapter 5. In the same way, jazz bands develop over the years; an excellent example is that of the Duke Ellington Orchestra. This was a small group, playing relatively simple pieces when it was formed in the mid-1920s. It developed impressively between that time and 1974, when Ellington died. The changes in Ellington's orchestra and music were sometimes gradual, sometimes quite rapid. The organization had its ups and downs, sometimes losing key musicians, but gaining new recruits too, people who enriched the orchestra with their talents. It also had to cope with the loss to the armed forces of several of its members during the war. This process of development, and the vicissitudes encountered along the way, bear many similarities to a family's long-term development.

A well-functioning family may be likened to a well-practiced band, whose musicians have played together for a long time, communicate well with one another, respect each others' roles and professional skills, understand the different functions of the members of the group, and have common objectives. Few, if any, instructions need be given to the musicians while such a band is playing. On the other hand, in a poorly functioning band there may be struggles for power, disagreements about the tempos at which tunes should be played, uncertainty about who has the final decision about what should be done when members disagree, competing desires to share the limelight, and a general lack of order and organization. When such problems exist the collective effort of the band suffers.

The rather sad story of Fletcher Henderson's band could be the framework for a metaphor for some of the things that can go wrong in a family. In that case more detail (which need not be factually correct in every respect and could be presented as what you "presume" went wrong) of the events in the band would probably need to be given. Bear in mind, though, that the promotion of insight into a problem seldom in itself causes the problem to be resolved. A useful approach, however, can be to discuss with family members what went wrong in the organization you are using as a metaphor—in this case the Henderson band. In this way, actions the group could have taken to improve its functioning can be identified. Indirectly the family would have gained ideas that they could apply to their own situation, perhaps without the connection even becoming conscious.

Rather than simply describe the Henderson band, another possibility is to contrast it with a successful band. Incorporated into the account of the successful band could be some metaphors for changes that the family might, with benefit, consider making.

ENMESHMENT AND DISENGAGEMENT

Families, or subsystems within families, are said to be *enmeshed* when the boundaries between individuals, or groups of individuals, are unclear and the people concerned are overinvolved with each other. The opposing terms *enmeshment* and *disengagement* were defined by Minuchin (1974), who pointed out that there is a continuum between the extremes they represent. All relationships fall somewhere along this continuum; there is no point at which the relationship becomes "abnormal" or pathological, although Minuchin believes that operations at either extreme may be indicators of pathology.

Enmeshed families, or family subsystems, may be distinguished by the way behavior (including the manifestations of emotional states) in one member of the enmeshed group—and especially *change* in behavior—has a very marked effect on other members of the group. Enmeshed subjects are specially sensitive to what is happening to those with whom they are enmeshed.

A common accompaniment of enmeshment is an absence of the clearly defined hierarchical relationships that exist within most families; related to this is a lack of clear boundaries between the family's subsystems. The result may be that the distinction between parent and child may be unclear, so that the parents fail to provide for their children the leadership, structure, and discipline children need for healthy development. It is not always helpful for everyone to be friends together, on an equal basis.

Disengagement exists when there is low sensitivity among family members to the needs, feelings, and behavior of other family members; there is thus little reaction among other members, or other subsystems of the family, to behavior that deviates from the family pattern or that may indicate emotional distress, pain, joy, or other feelings. In a disengaged family—or other group—the members are each wrapped up in their own concerns and interests, and have relatively little concern for the other family/group members.

What have jazz bands got to do with enmeshment and disengagement? Much or little, depending on whether the therapist is comfortable using them metaphorically. Therapists who are unfamiliar with jazz music may wish to choose other contexts for metaphors—football teams, surgical operating teams, or groups of workers engaged in the production or servicing of products. Milton Erickson told tales set in the kind of rural environment he grew up in, and he taught using metaphors drawn from his clinical practice. All of us, including the families we treat, have our areas of knowledge and interest and of ignorance, and we must take these factors into account in constructing the therapeutic metaphors we use. Thus it is simply because jazz bands interest me that they are used as carriers of metaphor here; there is nothing special about them.

By now it may be becoming clear to you how the metaphor of musicians playing together, whether in a jazz band or some other group, may be used to deal with problems of enmeshment and disengagement. Stories may be told about musical groups, the members of which were so enmeshed that confusion occurred. When a group of musicians is engaged in collective improvisation each must keep to his or her allotted role; when one is playing a solo, the accompanying musicians must adjust the volume of their instruments so as not to drown out what the soloist is playing. There is thus a need for clear boundaries between the members of the group; there also needs to be a clear boundary between the members and their leader, something that the quotation from Lawrence Lucie reproduced earlier in the chapter suggests did not exist in the Fletcher Henderson band.

Therapeutic metaphors are not usually devoted simply, or mainly, to offering camouflaged interpretations of what is happening in a clinical situation; they may also attempt to reframe situations, and to suggest solutions. Thus the excess zeal of a musician who consistently trespasses on fellow musicians' musical territory might be labeled an overabundance of youthful enthusiasm. In this "developmental reframing" (see Chapter 5), the erring band member is regarded as behaving in an immature fashion, rather than in a "bad" or "sick" one. Alternatively, or additionally, a story or anecdote about a successful band, in which all members played their allotted roles under sound leadership might be offered. The description of the qualities of the successful leader would constitute an offer of a possible solution, and parents might learn from such a description something of value to them in their roles as leaders within their family groups.

Disengagement, of course, can be tackled in a similar way, that is by describing bands—or sports teams, boards of directors, even treatment teams—in which there is too little involvement of the members with each other. It can also be reframed, for example, as a manifestation of exaggerated respect for the positions and areas of responsibility of others, or as a well-intentioned desire not to interfere in the affairs of colleagues.

Possible solutions to problems of disengagement can also be offered by metaphor. This may be done by devising a story or anecdote, isomorphic with the real-life people and scenario, about disengaged subjects who find a way of functioning more effectively by getting closer. To return to our jazz band, the importance of close cooperation between the musicians, with each one listening carefully to what the others are playing, to say nothing of starting off at the same tempo and in the same key, can easily be brought out in a short story. A tale of a rehearsal that went badly until the musicians realized the changes they needed to make in their musical relationships, might be helpful to certain families.

A family scapegoat is a person who takes on the burdens of the family, sacrificing his or her interests for the good of other family members. The term has biblical origins. Indeed the biblical account of the scapegoat's use must be one of the earliest recorded examples of the use of a metaphorical task or ritual. The scapegoat is described in Chapter 10 of the Book of Leviticus, which is itself a compendium of metaphorical tasks, from the making of thank offerings of grain, through the sacrificing of bulls and other animals, to fasting at prescribed times and for specific periods.

First, the scapegoat is selected, then Aaron, the priest, was to ''put both of his hands on the goat's head and confess over it all the evils, sins, and rebellions of the people of Israel, and so transfer them to the goat's head. Then the goat is to be driven off into the desert by a man appointed to do it. The goat will carry all their sins away with him into some uninhabited land'' (*Good News Bible*, 1976).

The problem with human scapegoats is that they do not usually depart into an uninhabited land—though they are sometimes committed to institutions—but instead tend to stick around. Actually, they generally serve a specific function in their families or other groups. (Scapegoats are not peculiar to families; they are to be found in schools, offices, board rooms, sports teams, committees—indeed anywhere people are gathered together and want someone to blame when things are going badly.)

A common clinical situation is one in which there is strife or more serious disagreement between the parents in a family. In such a family the role of the scapegoat may be to give the parents something to agree about. By behaving badly the child attracts the attention of the parents, thus distracting them from their own battles, which may remain largely covert. Less frequently, a similar function is served by a scapegoat's excessively good behavior; the role of "family angel" has been described by Gross (1979).

Metaphors for these roles are not hard to find, for scapegoats are to be found in virtually all social, political, vocational, and professional groups. In a jazz band, for example, one musician might be blamed for the failure of the group as a whole or for some section of it.

PROBLEMS OF ROLE ASSIGNMENT AND PERFORMANCE

In a well-functioning family all the tasks necessary to ensure the well-being of the family and its members are assigned to specific individuals who carry them out. This is not usually a formal, explicit process; the rules about who does what develop over the months and years, in most families without much discussion and without negotiations being consciously entered into by anyone. A pattern develops, and if some necessary functions are not performed someone steps into the breach and does whatever has to be done without a formal meeting being held to discuss the matter. An unwritten family rule, of which no one may be consciously aware, has come into play.

The roles played by the various family members depend on many factors which we need not explore here, but they can all be represented metaphorically. For example, the role a jazz drummer would expect to play on joining a band would depend upon that drummer's training and previous experience. The "training" could be presented as a metaphor for the subject's childhood experiences and rearing. Experience in other bands could represent the life in another family of a child now living in a "blended" family. The enlarging of the band by the addition of a new member could represent the birth of a baby, or the adoption of a child. Members leaving the family, falling ill, or dying, or parents separating—just about anything that can happen in a family can be represented by analogous events in a band.

Although the assignment and appropriate performance of roles are essential to the satisfactory performance of a jazz band, many North American families may find the metaphor of a football or hockey team more meaningful; in Britain a soccer team or a cricket team might serve better. (Metaphors should not only be isomorphic with the clinical situation; therapists will usually find it helpful to consider as well the culture within which they work and to choose scenarios that are meaningful to clients.) Whatever metaphorical situations they choose, however, therapists can devise scenarios in which roles either are clearly assigned or they are not, or in which certain team or band members perform idiosyncratic or dysfunctional roles, while perhaps others perform more functional roles. Using the principles and examples set out in earlier chapters, therapists will be able to construct isomorphic situations that will both help their clients understand how role assignment and performance might be improved in their families and point to possible ways of achieving these improvements. Along the way therapists will also be able to interpret and reflect the intentions of those whose performance is dysfunctional in a positive way, which can be therapeutically valuable.

Role confusion occurs when it is not clear to the members of a family what each one should be doing. The likely results include competition between certain members to perform certain tasks, while other functions are not performed at all or are done reluctantly, perfunctorily, and after much argument or open strife between members of the family.

In selecting metaphors for use when there is role confusion therapists may choose from among the metaphorical scenarios already mentioned, but many others are possible too. Another choice might be a poorly organized retail store, in which the buyers, stock controllers, personnel concerned with advertising, accounting staff, and sales personnel did not have properly developed job specifications so that they each did what they thought they should, and perhaps liked to do, to the detriment of the overall functioning of the store. Such a metaphor might make the point that the leadership provided by the joint owners of the store (if it was being offered to a two-parent family) was in some way unsatisfactory, if this appeared to be the case in the family concerned. Again, it would probably be helpful to use the metaphor to reframe the behavior of the staff concerned, emphasizing that they were all doing their best while operating in the system that existed in the store, and perhaps offering one or more possible solutions.

COMMUNICATION PROBLEMS

In many troubled families there are problems of communication.* Sometimes families, or marital couples, present, saying that they "can't communicate" or "don't communicate." Yet most therapists believe, along with Watzlawick and his colleagues (1967), that it is impossible not to communicate. Nonverbal messages, such as those transmitted by bodily posture and movement, are communicated constantly, and silence itself, or the refusal to answer questions carries its own message. The fact that communication is not entirely, or even mainly, verbal can readily be addressed metaphorically. Colleagues on almost any team enterprise who tend to express their feelings and thoughts nonverbally rather than verbally may form the subject of the metaphor.

Communications also define relationships. People speak differently according to whether they are asking, ordering, or pleading with others to do something. Respect, contempt, anger, approval, disapproval, and many other aspects of people's relationships are expressed by both the verbal and the nonverbal content of their communications. Communication may be *symmetrical*, which implies that the communicating persons are on an equal footing, or *complementary*, in which one person is in some way subordinate to the other, as in the teacher–student or penitent–confessor relationships. As Haley (1976) points out, communication can define the balance of power between two people.

Satir (1967, 1972) particularly emphasizes the communication

---

*See Barker (1981b), Chapters 3 and 5, for a discussion of communications theory and its importance in understanding how families function.

of feelings. How, and to what extent, family members communicate their feelings to each other are often crucial issues in troubled families. Many people who have self-image problems and difficulty with intimate relationships believe, rightly or wrongly, that their parents did not love them. Promoting the communication of such feelings can therefore be an important part of the treatment of some families.

All these aspects of communication can be illustrated and examined metaphorically, using any of the scenarios already mentioned, or others of one's choosing. For example, to deal with the question of how relationships between people are defined by the way they communicate, the therapist can tell stories in which people (or perhaps animals or fairy tale characters) hold conversations that define relationships. Such stories can be used to suggest solutions, promote insight, reframe situations, or even to deliver paradoxical directives, as in the following example.

William and Yvonne came seeking marital therapy. A striking feature of their case was the complementarity of their relationship. William, four years older than Yvonne, had always been in charge of the marital relationship. In the early years of the marriage this arrangement seemed to work, but now that the couple's two children had reached their teen years Yvonne was no longer satisfied with her role. William, though, was reluctant to cease being the leader and prime decision maker. He looked after the family finances, told Yvonne how much she could spend and on what, and made all the main decisions about the family's vacations, the children's education, and where the family should live.

Although the first few therapy sessions were useful in clarifying the couple's problem, little progress was made in making the marital relationship more symmetrical, which appeared essential if the marriage was to continue and Yvonne, a highly intelligent woman, was to get any satisfaction from it. The couple did not respond to direct injunctions, and several attempted strategic interventions failed to have much impact on them. Both, however, were good hypnotic subjects, and the following story was offered them under hypnotic trance. (The story could have been delivered without the use of hypnosis; the question of whether to use hypnosis when delivering metaphors is discussed in Chapter 11.)

You'll probably be interested in the story of King Oliver
and Louis Armstrong. It's a story from the early days of jazz,
when musicians were still developing and refining this particular art form.

Joe "King" Oliver was born in Louisiana in 1885, 15 years
before Armstrong. He lost the sight in one eye as a result
of an accident in early childhood. A cornet player, he led
a band in New Orleans in the early years of the century. In
1918 he was one of the first New Orleans band leaders to
move to Chicago.

Oliver's band achieved great success in Chicago, playing
for long periods at the Rose Garden Cafe. Although he had
vision in only one eye, Oliver was a perceptive man; the
competition in Chicago was hot, and he knew he had to
work hard to keep ahead of the musical game there. In 1922,
therefore, he sent for Louis Armstrong, a formidable young
musician from New Orleans, to join him on second cornet.
There was thus created, in its definitive form, the King Oliver Creole Jazz Band, one of the first New Orleans bands
to record and, many say, one of the greatest ever.

At first things went well. With two cornet players, the
band achieved a powerful sound. Oliver, the older and more
experienced musician, played the leading role, both in the
band and in the two-cornet team that played a key role in
it. He played most of the cornet solos, Armstrong playing
along with him during the ensembles. But Louis's musical
skills and creative powers grew steadily, until he became
at least as good a cornet player as Oliver.

For quite a while the young Louis Armstrong was content with his role. He worshiped "Mr. Joe" and, no doubt,
learned a lot from him. In time, though, he and Oliver had
to come to terms with their situation. Though he was the
younger man, musically they were equals. This was a hard
situation for them both. We can only speculate about the
pain they went through as they considered it. But things
cannot always remain the same; we all have to develop and
adjust to our situations as circumstances change. For a long
time Louis told people, "I can't quit Mr. Joe; Mr. Joe sent
for me and I can't quit him." But eventually he decided that
he, too, had to be a bandleader and Oliver's equal. Oliver
continued to lead fine bands during the remainder of the

1920s, while Armstrong went on to form his "Hot Five" and "Hot Seven" which, like the Oliver Creole Band, made jazz history.

This story, based on the account of Armstrong's life given by Jones and Chilton (1971), is rather wordy, and at one point a non sequitur—the statement that Oliver was perceptive despite having vision in only one eye—is introduced. These are devices that are useful in hypnotic work, but they can be helpful also when no attempt is made to induce trance; the irrelevant or illogical material may occupy the conscious mind while the unconscious mind absorbs the metaphorical message.

The delivery of this story seemed to help William and Yvonne redress the imbalance in their relationship. The emphasis was placed on the point that the two musicians remained in the music business, continuing as colleagues and becoming equals; the fact that they parted to lead separate bands was not emphasized, though it might have been if, for example, William and Yvonne had been engaged in running different businesses and there had appeared to be a need for each of them to operate more independently and autonomously—or at least to consider doing so. In delivering metaphors it is always desirable to mark out important points by, for example, speaking in a different voice, or more slowly or loudly. The fact that the two subjects of this tale became more equal was emphasized in this way.

The story could have been told with other emphases and interpretations. Thus Armstrong's departure from Oliver's band could be described in terms that present the process as more like a son's or daughter's emancipation from a parent at adolescence. For other purposes, Armstrong's wife, who was largely responsible for persuading Louis that it was time to leave Joe Oliver, could be brought into the story.

SUMMARY

Constructing metaphors for family problems is usually a more complex task than creating them for individual clients. Although full-length stories that address the total family situation in a comprehensive way are sometimes useful, in many cases shorter stories or other metaphorical devices designed to deal with certain limited aspects of families' functioning are a better approach. A series of metaphors, perhaps interspersed with other strategic devices, may be used to deal successively with the various aspects of the therapeutic task, so that treatment proceeds in stages.

In working with families, metaphors may be used to give the family members a better understanding of their situation, but they are often better employed to reframe situations and offer solutions. Virtually any situation in which people, animals, or fantasy figures work together in a collective endeavor may be used in the construction of metaphors for use with families. Therapists are usually wise, however, to select scenarios with which they are familiar.

A PRACTICAL EXERCISE

Mandy, aged 10 and an only child, has recently developed symptoms of school refusal. Her father, a successful businessman, is not much involved with Mandy and has left the task of getting Mandy to go to school to his wife. Mandy's mother has become increasingly concerned about the problem, but all her attempts to persuade, coax, coerce, and bribe Mandy into going to school have failed. Although all three members were asked to come when the family was referred to you, the father did not do so, telling his wife to say that he could not spare the time from his work. Whatever needed to be done to get Mandy to school, he had said, could be done by her mother.

By telephoning the father yourself you have managed to get him to come to the third therapy session, but he is unconvinced that there is any need for him to be involved in the task of getting Mandy back to school. How might you use a metaphorical approach to engage him in the therapy process, and to convince him of the need to work with his wife in helping to resolve Mandy's problem?

9

Metaphors and the Wider Social Context

Brett and Corinne owned a company that fabricated parts from lightweight alloys, principally for the aircraft industry. The company had not had an easy time in the past; many of their contracts had run into difficulties of various sorts, and at times Brett and Corinne came close to despair, wondering if they would ever make a success of their business. They were delighted, therefore, when they landed a contract to supply parts for the undercarriages of planes being built by one of the largest aircraft manufacturing companies in the country. It meant devoting nearly all the resources of their small factory to this one contract, but the future of the plane for which the parts were needed seemed secure; it seemed likely that this aircraft would remain in production for many years.

At first all went well. It took the owners some time, of course, to prepare their factory so that it could, and in a timely way, produce the parts needed. A considerable capital investment in new machinery was necessary. But Brett and Corinne had no doubt that they were making the right decision, even though it was a case of putting almost all their eggs in one basket.

146

Things proceeded on schedule and the parts the factory began producing were of good quality and conformed to the specifications of the aircraft manufacturer. The prospects for the small company seemed good.

Then one day a bombshell exploded in Brett's office: a letter arrived from the aircraft company, saying that it was terminating the contract. The letter was vague about the reasons but referred to "unsatisfactory relations" between the two companies.

Brett and Corinne were devastated and in a state of shock for the rest of the day. Everything they had worked for, and pinned their hopes on, seemed suddenly to have been destroyed. Efforts to telephone the relevant people at the aircraft manufacturers proved unsuccessful; everyone seemed to be "unavailable at present," and no one phoned them back. They felt betrayed and abandoned.

As the shock started to wear off, the dispirited factory owners experienced increasing feelings of anger. How could these people do this to them? They had always provided the aircraft company with a good quality product, delivered on time; indeed, for months they had devoted their whole lives to the project. They thought immediately of legal action and talked with their lawyer, who was as mystified about what had happened as were Brett and Corinne, though he thought there might be grounds for suing the larger company and recovering damages.

There was one person in the aircraft company with whom Brett had established a particularly good relationship; Don was in charge of the division responsible for purchasing components from outside manufacturers, and he had always seemed a reasonable and honest man. He was away the day the letter arrived, but was expected back the following Monday.

"Rather than sit here fuming with rage and discussing legal action," Brett said to Corinne, "I think we should get hold of Don next week and find out what has really been happening; perhaps he can help us decide what we can do about the situation."

"I suppose you're right," Corinne replied. "But the way I feel at the moment, I'd prefer to go and punch his face in."

Despite Corinne's reservations, the meeting with Don was duly set up. Brett and Corinne both went and were surprised to be met by a group of five executives. The atmosphere was cordial, if a little strained.

After introductions had been made and some small talk engaged in, a surprising story emerged about Eric, one of Brett's and Corinne's most trusted employees. This man was responsible for seeing that the parts were shipped to the aircraft firm in good condition and on time. He had always assured his employers that this was happening. It now emerged, though, that the parts had not always arrived on time, that the documentation required with them was frequently not in order, and that all sorts of weak excuses for the supplier's failure to perform were offered.

Corinne and Brett were flabbergasted. How could Eric have let them down in this way? They had always treated him well, and given him their respect and trust. Why would he have behaved in such a thoroughly irresponsible way? Did he have something against them? Was he mentally ill? And how could communication in their small company have been so poor that they didn't know what was going on?

Fortunately this meeting proved to be a turning point in the affairs of Brett's and Corinne's business. The problems between the two companies were sorted out to the satisfaction of both. Eric was interviewed and found to have a mass of personal problems of which neither Brett nor Corinne had had an inkling. He was offered, and accepted, some professional help and was later able to return to work in a different capacity.

THE SOCIAL CONTEXTS OF INDIVIDUALS AND FAMILIES

The family is the first important social environment we experience, and for some people it continues to be the prime social influence. But families also have their own social environments, and these often need to be considered during therapy. In addition, many people do not live as members of family groups, even though their families—or their memories and fantasies of them—may be important to them. A subgroup of this last category, one of particular interest to therapists who work with children and adolescents, is composed of children who have been removed from their families and are, often, in the care of child welfare agencies.

Metaphors can be particularly valuable in dealing with issues involving family groups or individuals and the wider social environment. Indeed, I have found that, in dealing with children in the care of child welfare agencies or placed long-term in institutions, metaphors can be especially useful. Such children often experience much pain and distress when their situations are discussed directly. Approaching them metaphorically in the first instance can be easier for them and may produce clinically better results.

METAPHORS FOR FAMILIES AND THEIR SOCIAL CONTEXTS

Among the institutions and groups with which families often have important relationships are schools, social agencies, neighborhood groups, other families, employers, and the police. Any of these relationships may need to be considered during therapy with families.

Tensions between families and the schools their children attend are common and may arise in various ways. The family, or certain members of it, may believe that the teachers are doing a poor job. Teachers may believe that a child's home environment is deficient in various ways and thus that it is adversely affecting a student's progress. Children may respond in very different ways in the two environments. And, finally, communication between family and school may be inadequate, distorted, or indirect, as, for example, when it occurs mainly through the children rather than directly between parents and school staff.

There are various ways of addressing these kinds of problems. The best plan is often to get everyone concerned with the problem together. This is sometimes difficult, but when the problem seems to reside in the relations between family and school, a meeting of all parties concerned can usually be arranged. And even when it proves impossible to involve everyone in the therapy process, a change in the attitudes, beliefs, and/or feelings of one or more of the parties may be sufficient to produce needed change in the system.

Happily for those of us who construct therapeutic metaphors, the world is full of examples of people, groups, or companies in conflict with other organizations or groups. Typically, the latter are larger and wield some sort of authority; for example government departments, school boards, and child welfare and other social agencies. The story at the beginning of this chapter, modified to be isomorphic with the situation of an actual family, could be used as a metaphor for such a situation. Suppose we had a family with a school-age child. The characters in real life might correspond with those in our metaphorical story as suggested in Table 4. The significant relationships and events in the real-life and metaphorical situations might correspond as indicated in Table 5.

Table 5 does not cover all the points made in the story; in the story, for example, Brett and Corinne are described as becoming very angry once the initial shock of getting the letter had worn

Table 4
Another Real-Life Family and
Its Metaphoric Counterpart

Real Life		Metaphor
Father	has become	Brett
Mother	has become	Corinne
The family	has become	Brett's and Corinne's business
One of the children	has become	Eric
The children's school	has become	The aircraft manufacturer
The children's teachers	have become	The executives at the aircraft company
The school counselor	has become	Don

Table 5
Another Metaphoric Scenario

Real Life	Metaphor
The family had had difficulties in the past.	The company had not had an easy time. Previous contracts had run into difficulties.
The parents had devoted great efforts to the care of their children.	All Brett's and Corinne's efforts went into making a success of this project.
One of the children deceived the parents into thinking that all was well at school.	Eric decieved his employers about the situation at the aircraft company.
The parents were deeply distressed when they learned that their child was in trouble at school.	Brett and Corinne were "devastated" when they heard they were to lose their contract.
The parents had a good relationship with the school counselor.	Brett and Corinne got on well with and trusted Don.
A face-to-face meeting with the school staff was required.	Brett and Corinne realized they had to meet with the aircraft company executives.
Once parents and school staff had all the facts and understood the situation properly, a construcuve plan for dealing with the child's problems could be developed.	When the misunderstandings between the two parties had been cleared up and they both had the full facts, a satisfactory solution to the problems was found.
Communication between parents and child was poor; improving it led to resolution of the problems.	Communication in Brett's and Corinne's company was poor; improving it was likely to help resolve the problems.

off. This point would probably be made only if the parents had indeed felt very angry at the equivalent point in the sequence of actual events. Similarly, the statement that Brett and Corinne considered taking legal action might be included only if the parents had themselves considered such action, although there might also be a case for including such a statement simply to emphasize how angry the parents were. The point, though, is that metaphors should be prepared with care, so that they are isomorphic with the real-life situation and do convey the message the therapist intends. You will readily see how the framework above could be modified to meet the needs of other cases.

A therapist may sometimes wish to suggest, by means of a metaphor, that a family might consider seeking help from a third party.

> Fred and Gail were approached by Hanna, a friend who asked them to sign for a television set she wanted to rent; apparently her credit rating wasn't good, but she assured them that if they signed for the set she would make the monthly payments. Unfortunately she didn't, and she also refused to return the set, either to Fred and Gail or to the store from which it was rented.
>
> Eventually there seemed no alternative but to have the store repossess the set. Fred agreed to pay the legal costs involved in getting the appropriate court order. This was duly obtained, but when the Sheriff's officers went to get the set they discovered that the serial number that had been provided by the store and was on the court order was not the one on the set. Rectifying this and getting a new order from the court took several weeks and involved further legal costs.
>
> Fred told the manager of the rental company that he was not prepared to pay the additional costs arising from their having misquoted the television set's serial number. But when the set was finally repossessed, the company nevertheless sent him a bill that included all the legal costs, including those incurred in rectifying their error. When he queried this, the manager of the rental company declined to discuss the matter and insisted he pay the full amount for which he had been billed. Fred refused and deducted what he considered a fair sum from the bill.
>
> There followed a series of further bills and threatening letters from the company. Fred and Gail were told they

would be reported to the Credit Bureau and that their credit file would be marked as an "unpaid collection." Their file, they were informed, would be checked each time they applied for credit, whether to buy a car, open a credit card account, or even rent an apartment because, one of the letters said, landlords usually check the credit ratings of those wanting to rent from them. On top of that they were also threatened with court action.

Naturally the couple were quite upset. Gail took the threats especially seriously, envisaging all sorts of financial and legal disasters befalling them. For a while they debated what to do. Then a friend suggested they call the Better Business Bureau.

Fred took the friend's advice. He found himself speaking to a very helpful person who immediately understood the situation.

"What you should do," she said, "is write to the Credit Bureau and explain that yours is a 'disputed account'; you should ask them to mark your file accordingly when they receive the complaint from the television rental company. You should also send the rental company a letter, by registered mail, explaining why you do not consider that you owe the money they are demanding."

The Better Business Bureau representative went on to explain that there was nothing Fred could do to prevent a collection agency from attempting to obtain money the company alleged it was owed. The agency staff might threaten them and emotionally harass them, but they could take no other action to obtain payment without a court order. If the matter came to court it would be in the Small Claims Court, and Fred would have the opportunity to explain his case directly to the judge; he would not need to hire a lawyer.

When Fred heard all this he felt much better; he went home and explained the situation to Gail, who also felt much relieved. [It can sometimes be helpful to seek outside expert advice when you're in difficulty, or when you think you may be, and it may even be surprising to you how often you can get this for free, as Fred did from the Better Business Bureau.]

The final sentence, in square brackets, might or might not need to be included. If the metaphor were delivered to a subject in a state of hypnotic trance, it probably would not be necessary; in trance the unconscious mind seems to be able to make metaphorical connections more easily, and the conscious mind seems less critical and questioning. In the normal alert state, however, it sometimes helps to make the point of the story a little clearer so that the subject's conscious mind understands it too—though even in such situations it is probably the unconscious processes and changes that really matter.

INDIVIDUALS AND THEIR SOCIAL CONTEXTS

Much of what has been said about the relationships between families and their social settings applies also to individuals and *their* social settings. It would not be hard, for example, to modify the two stories already set out in this chapter for use with individuals.

Individuals are often at a disadvantage when they are dealing with large and powerful organizations such as governments, corporate employers, or social agencies. Joining together with others who are similarly situated can be helpful; individuals working together in a group can assist and support each other, so that they all deal with their problems better.

When devising metaphors for individuals who are having difficulty dealing with larger systems, you may find that the "self-help" movement can provide what you require. Quite apart from the fact that there may exist self-help groups that can assist your clients, stories about such groups and how useful they have been to others may plant in clients' minds ideas about getting together with others who face similar problems. Anecdotes such as the following may be useful in these.

> When I worked in England one of the things that impressed me was the help many parents, and also quite a number of children, received from the British Epilepsy Association. It can be quite a blow for parents to learn that their

child has epilepsy. But, although children with epilepsy and their families do face a number of problems, being part of a group of people with the same problem seemed to be a real help to many of the families. It was good to see how the parents of these children joined with others who also had epilepsy to obtain information about the condition— how to handle it, what resources were available in the community to deal with it, and who the experts were and where they were to be found. It also seemed helpful to these families to meet others in the same boat and to compare experiences, especially the various ways they had dealt successfully with the problems that epilepsy can pose. The families seemed to obtain emotional support as well as factual information, and both seemed to help them.

There was also in Britain a remarkably successful society for autistic children. It was a politically active and effective lobby group; it succeeded in getting schools and classes for autistic children set up in various parts of the country, and it ran at least one school of its own. I'm sure the benefits to the children were great, but I was impressed also by the way getting together helped the parents. It seemed to enable them to overcome many of the emotional and other problems that can so easily develop when you're faced with the sort of difficult behavior autistic children often show.

After being told such anecdotes clients sometimes ask directly about available self-help groups, and there is no reason why they should not be given any information the therapist has available. On the other hand, you will probably not need to use anecdotes about self-help groups when you are dealing with clients who are initially open to seeking outside help. Such anecdotes are of value principally when you are dealing with individuals, or families, who are reluctant to seek the help of others in similar situations, perhaps because they feel embarrassed, ashamed, or even guilty about their problem. For such people, the more stories you tell about others who have been helped in analogous situations, or about groups that have supported their members in welcoming and nonjudgmental ways, the more likely you are to help them become open to such help themselves.

CHILDREN IN FOSTER CARE

Children in the care of child welfare agencies are often particularly difficult to treat. Although they may have serious emotional problems with which they need help, for many reasons they can be hard to reach. Children who have been removed from the care of their parents have often been subjected to a whole series of unrewarding or downright damaging relationships and experiences; these may include physical and sexual abuse, repeated rejections by parents and others who should have been caring for them, and multiple moves from one home to another. It is not uncommon to find that, after being taken from their natural homes, children have been moved repeatedly from one living situation to another, including foster homes, group homes, and institutions.

It is not surprising that many children and adolescents who are wards of the state are suspicious of adults, particularly of those who try to adopt a caring role. These young people feel let down by those they once trusted. Adolescents tend to be especially suspicious because they have usually been subject to the stresses described for longer than younger children. Teenagers' suspiciousness, moreover, may be compounded by the rebelliousness that is often seen even in adolescents whose development is proceeding along more normal lines.

In treating this difficult clinical group, indirect methods of communication and strategic approaches to promoting change are often helpful. Indeed, the therapist who chooses to work with these young people needs to have available a wide range of therapeutic strategies and skills. Among these skills, familiarity with the use of metaphor should probably be given a high rating.

In treating children who are wards of the state, a number of issues may require special consideration:

1. The child's or young person's mistrust of adults and of the entire child welfare system.
2. The multiple rejections these children have often suffered.
3. The feelings of despair and hopelessness that these children in care often experience.

4. The feelings of low self-esteem that are characteristic of children who have been wards of the state for a long time.
5. Problems in the relationships between the child or adolescent and the child welfare staff.

Relations between children who are wards of the state and staff members of child welfare agencies are often troubled. Children may have angry or ambivalent feelings toward their social workers who, they may feel, have taken them away from parents they love and placed them where they do not want to be. These feelings, of course, often represent displaced anger toward the natural parents, but children require help with them whether or not this is the case. Moreover, social workers, residential child care staff, foster parents, and others who deal with these children may also experience, and need help in dealing with, feelings of anger, exasperation, or despair.

METAPHORS FOR CHILDREN INVOLVED
WITH CHILD WELFARE AGENCIES

Metaphors are no panacea for these children, but therapists who treat this large and important group of clients—who are at great risk for emotional difficulties in adult life—may find them helpful when direct interventions prove ineffective. Some metaphorical approaches to each of the issues mentioned in the last section will therefore be outlined. These suggestions may be helpful to therapists in developing their own personal metaphors for the clinical situations described and for others like them.

Children's distrust of adults generally and of those in the child welfare system in particular is often hard to overcome, despite the fact that social workers and others are almost invariably trying to help the children and families in their care. Unfortunately the more distrustful and suspicious the children get the harder it is for the workers in the system to communicate with them and thus to help them effectively.

In such situations, stories about animals or people who frighten away those who try to help them, to treat their injuries, or even

just to feed them can be useful. Zoos are good places in which
to set such stories. In a zoo some animals are friendly and therefore get a lot of attention from the staff, but others are suspicious
and angry so that the staff don't go near them unless they absolutely have to.

A young person might be told about an angry tiger who found
he was getting no attention and decided, as an experiment, not
to roar angrily at the keeper every time he approached. This tiger,
it might be explained, was quite surprised to find that the keeper
then became more attentive and kind, brought him extra food,
and spent more time in his company. Even though the keeper
had the tiger locked up in a cage, the keeper didn't seem to mean
him any harm, the tiger decided; he even appeared to be trying
to help him.

Children in the welfare system often feel as if they are confined. And indeed they are often placed in situations that are not
of their own choosing, and sometimes they are literally locked
up in "secure" institutions. The metaphor of an angry, caged
animal is therefore often quite apt.

The multiple rejections children in the welfare system have often
suffered can also be represented metaphorically in stories about
animals; for example, pets that have been moved from home to
home or have been mistreated. The confinement of animals in
kennels and pounds can be used as a metaphor for the placement
of children in institutions.

As this chapter is being written, Canada's Province of Alberta
is conducting a public inquiry into a series of tragic circumstances
involving a 17-year-old youth who, after being a ward of the province for 14 years, killed himself. During that time this boy had
been in 16 approved foster homes, two unapproved foster homes,
and six group homes. The case, and the inquiry, has received
much public attention and extensive media coverage, so that
many young people in care became aware of it.

I have found it useful to discuss this boy's case with other
young people in the welfare system, for many of his experiences
parallel their own. His possible feelings and thoughts can be discussed as a metaphor for how they have felt, or are currently feel-

ing, about their situations. A conversation along these lines can go on to explore what young people in such situations can do to get help, how such help could be used if offered, and also what the child welfare service has learned as a result of the case under inquiry. What would things have been like for Richard if he had had a therapist willing to see him regularly and to act as an advocate as well as a counselor? What if he had had a social worker who knew how important it was to avoid frequent moves from one home to another, something workers now understand much better?

It is thus possible to use current events, even events as tragic as those leading to a 17-year-old's suicide, for their potential metaphorical meaning; things that are currently hot topics for public discussion, and are known to be real events that have happened locally, may have particular power as metaphors.

The feelings of despair and hopelessness experienced by many children in the welfare system may also need to be acknowledged metaphorically. This can be done by stories about prisoners in dungeons, miners trapped underground, or animals cornered by those hunting them, and by exploring how these characters felt in these situations. Such stories can then tell about the various ways the characters who felt despairing and helpless overcame those feelings and rose to the challenges of the occasions. By these means it is possible to offer hope to the hopeless and, sometimes, to suggest to clients ways in which they may deal creatively with the dilemmas they face, and so overcome their problems.

The feelings of low self-esteem that characterize many children who are wards of the state can be tackled by any of a number of approaches. Ways of enhancing self-esteem are discussed in Chapter 10.

The relations between children and adolescents in the welfare system and their social workers can be represented metaphorically using the relations between animals in a zoo and their keepers, between soldiers and their officers, between factory or office workers and the security personnel at the premises in which they work, or between members of a soccer team and their coach. Which, if any, of these you will choose in a particular case will depend on your understanding of your client's feelings. Does the child feel more like an animal or a soldier, or a soccer player? It helps also to have a sense of the child's understanding of what animals in a zoo, or soldiers subject to orders and discipline, and so forth, feel like. These are things that can be explored with the child prior to offering the metaphor.

Once you have chosen the metaphorical setting, the stories or anecdotes you use can be adapted to suit the needs of the particular case. Keepers in zoos, or security guards, or teachers, can be kind or mean, caring or uncaring, empathic or distant, consistent or inconsistent, flexible or inflexible—they can be subject to any polarity you care to name. Relationships with them can have various results, and anecdotes and longer stories can be structured to show how such characters respond differently according to how they are treated. Indeed, you can construct for some children a whole new reality—that is a whole new view of the child welfare system of which they are a part—through the telling of suitable stories with metaphorical meanings.

SUMMARY

Families and individuals have important relationships with the wider social systems of which they are part. When they are dealing with large organizations or agencies, including schools and child welfare agencies, they may be at a particular disadvantage. Metaphorical representations of these situations are readily constructed and may be useful in therapy with clients who have problems in these relationships. Metaphors may be used to help families and individuals find solutions or to try approaches they have not previously considered.

Children in the care of child welfare agencies often present especially challenging therapeutic problems. Because the agency is the legal guardian and, through the child's own social worker, must carry out most parental responsibilities, the relationship between the child and the usually large and sometimes bureaucratic agency is very important. But repeated abuse, whether physical, sexual, or verbal, may have left these children with feelings of guilt, despair, and hopelessness, with poor self-images, and with distrust of the adult world. Therapeutic approaches to these problems require much skill and understanding; because of the delicate nature of the relationships, and the intense emotions they may evoke, indirect approaches, particularly those involving metaphors, are often best.

A PRACTICAL EXERCISE

Audrey is 15 years old. A native North American girl, she was adopted into a family of Anglo-Saxon origin at the age of 4. At 11 she started to rebel against her adoptive parents' rules, and she then embarked on a long career of running away from home and getting involved in delinquent activities and the use of drugs. She has now been in the care of the child welfare service for nearly three years. She has had three social workers and has been in a "receiving home" (a temporary placement for children when they are first taken into care), two foster homes, a group home, and an adolescent treatment center. Currently she is in the juvenile detention center, waiting to appear in court. She recently ran away from the treatment center and, in the company of two boys, broke into several houses.

Audrey is a girl of superior intelligence and excellent verbal skills. Currently she is in a very angry mood; she says she is always being moved around, her new social worker (whom she has had for only three weeks) doesn't understand her and has only been to see her twice, the treatment center isn't helping her, and she isn't sure whether her adoptive parents want her back—or whether she would want to go back if they did. She wonders if she should try and find her natural mother and asks you if you can help her do this. Alternatively, she says, perhaps she should kill herself and she has in the past slashed her wrists.

Audrey disqualifies any attempts you make to discuss her situation rationally and directly. Devise a series of metaphorical approaches that might help her see some positive things about her situation and tackle her problems more constructively.

10

Miscellaneous Uses of Metaphor

DICK WHITTINGTON'S REMARKABLE RISE
TO FAME AND FORTUNE

Richard, usually known as Dick, Whittington was born about 1358 in Pauntley, Gloucestershire, England. His parents died when he was young and he had a difficult time as a child. He ran wild about the countryside, often went hungry, wore ragged clothes, and slept wherever he could find a place to lay his head. The village folk gave him scraps of food and helped him out when they could, but they were poor too.

Dick was a smart boy, despite his poor circumstances, and he kept hearing tales about London, the streets of which, people said, were paved with gold. So one day Dick hitched a ride to London with a man whose wagon was pulled by eight fine horses, all with bells at their heads. The wagoner was at first reluctant to take the boy, but when he heard that Dick had no parents and saw how ragged his clothes were, and how hungry he looked, he thought he could be no worse off in London.

It was a long, slow journey to London, but at last they reached the great city's gates. Dick thanked the wagoner and ran into the big city. Alas, there was no gold to be seen on the streets or anywhere else Dick went! When night came Dick, tired and hungry, curled up in an alleyway and cried himself to sleep.

When he awoke, Dick, a country boy, was amazed at the din and clutter of the city; he'd seen and heard nothing like it before. He wandered around and tried asking people for food; many told him to go and find work, but he had no idea how to do this.

During the following days Dick almost starved to death. Then one day, feeling faint and ill, he curled himself up in the entrance to a big house just off a street called Cheapside which, despite its name, was an area where wealthy people lived. The cook found him and was about to send him away when the owner of the house, Mr. FitzWarren, a wealthy merchant, came along. He took pity on the boy, invited him into his house and told the servants to give him a good meal. He and his wife decided to employ Dick as a scullery boy, in return for his board and lodgings.

Dick was grateful for being given shelter and a bed to sleep on in the attic, but his room was infested with rats, which ran over him all night, and the cook gave him a very hard time, beating him mercilessly for the tiniest misdeeds, real or imagined.

One day a visitor gave Dick a penny for cleaning his boots. Dick at once went out and bought a cat; he kept the cat in his room, and fed it on scraps from the kitchen. It soon got rid of the rats. But Dick found he couldn't stand the cook's treatment of him any longer. So he decided to run away. Taking his cat, he stole away in the middle of the night. He got as far as Highgate Hill, where nowadays stands the Whittington Hospital, and sat down to rest. Then he heard the sound of the bells of Bow Church. They seemed to say,

> Turn again Whittington
> Lord Mayor of London.

"Lord Mayor of London!" thought Dick. "Surely I could never be that."

But something told Dick he could make it. He turned back and was busy scrubbing Mr. FitzWarren's kitchen when the cook got up. Dick had another lucky break when Mr. Fitz-Warren's trading ship, the *Unicorn*, was about to sail for foreign parts. It was the custom for the servants each to give the captain something to sell or barter when the ship reached its destination. But Dick, when asked what he would send, said he had nothing.

"My only possession is my cat," he told Mr. FitzWarren.

"Then fetch the cat and send it," said his master.

Dick did as he was told. Fortunately Miss Alice, the Fitz-Warrens' daughter, took pity on him and gave him money to buy another cat. Meanwhile the *Unicorn* set sail but was blown off course by gales and contrary winds. Eventually it came to the Barbary coast. This place was inhabited by the Moors, a dark-skinned people who had never seen English sailors before. Fortunately they proved friendly and keen to trade. They even invited the captain and crew to a meal. But as soon as the food was served, a host of rats appeared and devoured most of it. The Moorish king said he would give half his fortune to get rid of the rats; at once the captain thought of Dick's cat and sent for it.

It didn't take long for the cat to rid the king's palace of rats, so in exchange the king gave the captain the treasure he'd promised. When they had finished trading their goods with the Moors, the Unicorn's crew brought the ship home and the captain presented Mr. FitzWarren and his servants with the goods they had obtained. Dick was overwhelmed by his enormous share and wanted his master to take it. But Mr. FitzWarren refused, saying it was Dick's.

So Dick rewarded the sailors generously with gifts, and also gave presents to all the other servants—even the cook! Then he bought himself new clothes, had his hair cut by the best barber and resolved to use his fortune for the good of the people of London, especially the poor. He bought his own house, became Miss Alice's suitor and later married her, and was three times Lord Mayor of London: in 1397–1399, 1406–1407 and 1419–1420. He prospered in his various businesses, was a friend of three kings of England and lent Henry V money when the monarch was in need of funds. He did many good works, but he and Alice had no children.

When he died he left money for the rebuilding of Newgate Prison, to replace the old, notorious hell-hole. He also founded other charities, some of which continue to this day.

ENHANCING SELF-ESTEEM

In my office I have a poster; it has a deep blue background, against which is set the silhouette of a tree with bare branches. Visible through the tree's branches is a large, bright, full moon. In the top right-hand corner of the poster are the words, "Limits exist only in your mind."

This is a very suitable poster for a psychiatrist's office. Many people who seek the help of psychiatrists and their colleagues in the other mental health disciplines are experiencing problems in living because they believe that they do not have the resources they need to meet the challenges with which they are confronted. This lack of sufficient self-esteem characterizes many emotionally and behaviorally disturbed children as well as many adults. Low self-esteem can have some most unfortunate consequences, ranging from chronic academic and vocational underachievement, through delinquency and crime to depression and suicide. Steffenhagen (1983) considers low self-esteem an important etiological factor also in alcoholism, addiction to other drugs, and anorexia nervosa. It is a serious problem.

Some people whose self-esteem is low make no secret of that fact, but others use various mental defense mechanisms to deal with it and, at the conscious level, to deny it. Among these mechanisms are denial, reaction formation, projection, and displacement.

There is no absolute standard by which an individual's worth can be judged. For practical purposes we are what we believe we are, and often the therapist's task is to change clients' beliefs concerning who they are and what they can do.

The challenge we face, then, is to develop our skills in helping people change their opinions of themselves, opinions that they may have held from early childhood. Over the years these deeply felt views of themselves have probably been reinforced repeatedly, both by parents and by others who have told these troubled individuals they are "no-good kids" (or adults), and by unconsciously motivated failure in various areas of their lives.

What does a therapist do for an intelligent young woman who steals, lies, drinks excessively, uses a variety of street drugs, works as a prostitute, and considers herself worthy of nothing more than the violent, abusive pimp, currently in jail on a murder charge, with whom she is in love? She has a history of gross family instability, rejection by her alcoholic, abusive parents, sexual abuse, and a succession of placements in foster homes, group homes, and institutions. Her life has been a series of rejections and, deep down if not consciously, she feels both worthless and angry. Brief periods of relief from the emotional pain of her existence are obtained by getting "high" on alcohol or other drugs. The likelihood is that she will not even consider it worthwhile seeking treatment, because, deep down inside her, she *knows* she is good for nothing better than what she is doing. She is wrong, of course, but does not yet know it. She is unlikely to seek therapy of her own accord, and she will probably be seen professionally only if she is referred by a court or an agency (perhaps a probation officer), or finds herself in a drug treatment or alcohol detoxification center.

People like this are a real therapeutic challenge. They fit perfectly into the *DSM-III* category of "antisocial personality" (see *Diagnostic and Statistical Manual of the American Psychiatric Association*, 1980), a type of psychiatric disorder regarded as one of the most difficult to treat. Such people are a tantalizing group of individuals; if only they could come to believe that they could do something better or could live happily without drugs and alcohol, and that they need not be in and out of jail, the potential they possess to lead rich, rewarding lives could be realized. Their problems are essentially their self-images.

When people with self-images as poor as that of the young woman mentioned above have come my way, I have found that dealing directly with them—that is, telling them they have great potential and are well able to live happier, less dangerous, and generally more satisfying lives—has proved ineffective. Some form of indirect, strategic approach is usually needed if there is to be any change. The use of metaphorical methods is one approach that is sometimes effective.

Milton Erickson always maintained a strong belief in his patients' potential for healthy functioning. He was much less interested in exploring their psychopathology than in helping them obtain access to the resources within them. He could also see much of value in the experience of adversity. One of his "teaching tales" starts with the words,

> "We learn so much at a conscious level and then we forget what we learn and use the skill. You see, I had a terrific advantage over others. I had polio, and I was totally paralysed, and the inflammation was so great I had a sensory paralysis too." (Erickson quoted in Rosen, 1982, p. 47)

Here we have an interesting metaphor. It can be a "terrific advantage" to have been totally paralyzed! But why? And how? Because you learn so much in overcoming such a handicap, in surmounting adversity. The deprived, rejected child at least learns how children should not be brought up. Erickson never fully recovered from his first attack of poliomyelitis, and he was substantially handicapped after his second attack, at the age of 51. Yet he led a notably successful life.

Many of us who have suffered adversity—and who has not?—tend to seek refuge in self-pity. We cannot succeed because this, that, or the other thing has happened to us. Metaphors designed to assist clients to abandon this way of thinking will usually be stories of people who have triumphed over adversity. Erickson was certainly such a person, but his story may not appeal to all clients. Another was Corrie Ten Boom, a Dutch woman who survived a German concentration camp, and was moved by her experiences there to become a great preacher. Her story (*A Prisoner and Yet* . . . , Ten Boom, 1954), may particularly appeal to clients with Christian beliefs. Another concentration camp survivor who was able to surmount his experience and to draw useful material from it is the therapist and author, Victor Frankl (1962). Then there is Charlie Chaplin (1964), who overcame some adverse childhood experiences, including periods in Lambeth Workhouse, London, and the Hanwell Schools for Orphans and Destitute Children, to have an outstandingly successful career. Interestingly, Chaplin chose to play the role of clown, perhaps a reflection of his view of himself. Nevertheless, his story might be used as yet another example of how people can turn whatever resources they have to advantage.

Louis Armstrong's story provides a striking illustration of how adversity can be overcome. According to the account of his life given by the jazz historians, Max Jones and John Chilton (1971), he faced just about every difficulty possible as a child. He rarely saw his father and was brought up at various times by his mother, his older sister, and his grandmother, on the streets of New Orleans and in a Waifs Home, to which he was committed for discharging a gun in the streets.

Armstrong was born and spent his early years in a shack in James Alley; this has been described as "the lowest negro slum in New Orleans." "Dingy and dangerous, the whole area [was] peopled with an abnormally high percentage of toughs, robbers and 'women walking the streets for tricks'" (Jones & Chilton, 1971). He did not even have the advantage of a musical family background, though he must have had much innate musical talent. Armstrong is a good example of a person who, despite an extraordinarily adverse childhood, rose to fame and fortune.

And there is Dick Whittington. The story as told above is part fairy tale, part fact. It is based on the retelling of the tale by Kathleen Lines (1970). The truth is that we know almost nothing of Whittington's childhood, or indeed of his life before he became a prominent and wealthy Londoner, but he *was* three times Mayor of London and he did do much for the poor and founded various charities which exist to this day. It is quite easy therefore, in telling his story, to make it fit your therapeutic purposes by providing your own, tailor-made account of his childhood, isomorphic with that of your client.

You will have your own favorite stories, either true or fictional, about people who overcame adversity, and even used it to advantage. It is best to use stories you are familiar with and about people you especially admire. You will then speak with more conviction than you may about stories, for instance, that I have recounted here. The point is that stories like the foregoing can inspire people to attempt what may hitherto have seemed impossible to them.

So the first step in helping someone with a poor self-image is to deal with the skeleton in the closet—the person's conviction that as a result of past experiences he or she is destined to remain the same. This idea, incidentally, seems to be derived in part from a superficial knowledge of psychoanalytic theory, leading to the notion that the personality is formed early in childhood and cannot change thereafter. It is ironic that a theory developed as a basis for psychotherapy, a change-promoting process, should have come to have this counter-therapeutic effect. The story of Joe (Erickson, 1980e), which was summarized in Chapter 3, can often be useful in offering hope to people who believe that discontinuous change is impossible, and that change can only come about gradually, if at all.

People with poor self-images do not need only to free themselves from the idea that their past experiences have doomed them to failure, or at least to a limited choice of possibilities in life. They need also to realize that they have within them the resources necessary to achieve just about anything they wish. This may seem like a revolutionary, even absurd, statement. Can *anyone* succeed at *anything*? Perhaps not, but I would hesitate to tell anyone who is intent enough on success that he or she *cannot* succeed in achieving any particular ambition. After all, Dick Whittington was an unlikely enough prospect to become Lord Mayor of London even once, let alone three times, when he arrived penniless in the big city! True, he had a couple of lucky breaks, but he made good use of them, something we can all choose to do or not to do when good fortune comes our way. And Louis Armstrong, when he was committed to the Waif's Home at the age of 12, probably did not seem to have a very hopeful future.

In treating people with poor self-images, therefore, we need metaphors that carry the message that they have available within themselves resources of which they have previously been unaware. Erickson's concept of the unconscious as a great storehouse of "learnings"—that is, things we have learned but no longer remember learning—is useful in achieving this objective. It is itself a metaphor.

Erickson frequently used a subject's learning of the letters of the alphabet as an example of something the subject had learned but forgotten learning. He also incorporated it into the conversational induction of hypnotic trance, as transcribed in the book *Hypnotic Realities* (Erickson, Rossi, & Rossi, 1976). Early in the induction process he would say,

> "When you first went to kindergarten, grade school, this matter of learning letters and numerals seemed to be a big insurmountable task. . . . To recognize the letter A . . . to tell a Q from an O was very, very difficult. And then too, script and print were so different. But you learned to form a mental image of some kind. You didn't know it at the time, but it was a permanent mental image." (Erickson, Rossi, & Rossi, 1976, pp. 6–7)

In other words, the subject has learned many things that have been consciously forgotten but are nevertheless stored away in the "unconscious mind," available for use when needed. Knowledge of the letters of the alphabet is of course needed often, but we use the information stored in the unconscious quite automatically and without having to make any deliberate effort to gain access to it.

There are many other things we have learned and consigned to our unconscious minds. Erickson refers to them as "mental images." If we have ever been happy, or felt self-confident, or handled a particular type of situation well, we have the mental image of how to do this stored away in our unconscious minds, just as the knowledge of the shapes of the 26 lower-case letters, the 26 capital letters, and the 10 numbers from one to nine are stored there. These images are our resources, our unconscious psychological resources, with which to tackle the world and achieve fulfillment of our aims.

OTHER RESOURCE METAPHORS

In addition to the previously mentioned metaphorical approaches to helping people understand that they have more going for them than they think, certain images are often useful in promoting such ideas. These can be presented as straightforward analogies, they can be embedded in stories, or they can be used in the course of hypnotherapy.

One useful image is that of a storage cupboard or shed in which gadgets, tools, pieces of equipment, and materials are stored when they are not currently needed. Some items remain there for many years and may be forgotten. They are still there and available for use, even though their owner may have forgotten their existence and may not even remember what their original purpose was. In fact, such a cupboard or shed can become, over a period of years, a rich storehouse of useful things, and its owner may be surprised to discover how many resources are available there.

A similar image that may serve as a useful metaphor is that of a bank, or perhaps the bank's safety deposit service. Here, too, a person deposits valuable and useful things; in fact people often store their most valuable possessions in banks. Banks can therefore serve as metaphors for our unconscious minds, where we build up, over a period of years, a vast collection of resources that we can bring out of storage and into use when we need to do so.

I have occasionally mentioned to clients my fairly large record collection. This numbers some 1500 albums and, together with a fair-sized collection of audiocassettes, constitutes a substantial musical resource. But there are so many records and cassettes, some of them going back as far as 30 years, that it is hard to remember exactly what is available to play. Sometimes it is a great surprise to find records that prove to be just right for a particular mood or occasion.

All these images can be incorporated into stories, or they can be linked to ideas about resources available in the unconscious mind during hypnotherapy. In trance, it seems easier for people to associate ideas such as the storing of valuables in a bank and the accumulation of psychological resources in the unconscious mind.

This section would not be complete without reference to Milton Erickson's emphasis on his patients' "body images." Erickson's varied approaches to the changing of people's self-images are reviewed by Lankton and Lankton (1983, Chapter 8), and there are numerous examples to be found also in *Uncommon Therapy* (Haley, 1973). Study of these sources will assist therapists in devising metaphors to help increase patients' self-esteem, as well as suggesting other ways of achieving this end.

ENURESIS AND ENCOPRESIS

Diurnal and nocturnal enuresis are often found to be unassociated with organic disease. It is not always easy to discover why a child has failed to learn bladder control; it seems that in most cases it results from a combination of factors. These may include genetic predisposition, less-than-optimal toilet training by parents, and a high level of anxiety in the child. Sometimes wetting appears to be an expression of unconscious feelings of aggression, and occasionally it may present as willful defiance of parents or others. In addition, physical factors are occasionally responsible.

Similar considerations apply to encopresis, except that physical factors are more often found to play a part in encopresis than in enuresis. The most common physical factor is chronic constipation, although this is sometimes secondary to an emotionally determined refusal to defecate. In these cases the child's resistance to passing feces leads to a gradual build-up of hard fecal masses in the large intestine, where they may then become impacted. The muscle tone in the intestinal wall becomes impaired, and normal defecation is no longer possible; ''overflow inconti-nence'' then sets in, with loose, liquid feces leaking around the impacted masses. Physical treatment is now necessary, even though the problem was originally psychogenic and emotional factors still require treatment.

Fuller accounts of enuresis and encopresis are to be found in *Basic Child Psychiatry* (Barker, 1983). The foregoing points are mentioned here because psychotherapeutic methods of treating these symptoms, whether they employ metaphor or not, should not be instituted until the child's physical state has been appraised and any necessary treatment of physical problems has been car-ried out or is under way.

When psychological factors contribute to the causation of either enuresis or encopresis, as they often do, psychotherapeutic meth-ods are usually indicated in their treatment. Metaphor may be useful as part of this process, when the indications for its use, as set out in Chapter 2, are met. The following case, described by the child's therapist, provides an illustration.

Trevor, an eight-year-old foster child, had had a chronic and severe problem of diurnal enuresis for many years. There was no evidence of any underlying physical disease, but Trevor had had an unsettled life, with early physical abuse. He was taken into foster care as a baby, later returned to his mother, then taken into care again. He had been in many foster homes.

A shy, timid, anxious, and insecure boy, Trevor's fre-quent accidents in school and on the playground were a con-stant source of shame and embarrassment to him. Behav-ioral treatment approaches had been singularly unsuccessful in bringing about any diminution of the symptom. Trevor was also sensitive about his small build and size which, to him, implied weakness. In one therapy session, when he was more verbal and spontaneous than usual, Trevor de-scribed some of his feelings of self-consciousness about his size, particularly when people took him to be much young-er than he was, or when he was teased. We spoke about strength and how muscles and bones, though small, can still be very strong. I pointed out that some muscles are larger than others, and that even those that are small can be made stronger with practice, like "the one down at the bottom of the stomach" (to Trevor the whole abdomen was "the stomach").

When I made this remark Trevor quickly interjected that whenever he had to go to the bathroom he thought of a door. He just wanted to keep it shut. I casually directed his attention to my office door, and to the two tiny bolts which held it firmly and securely shut. We both marveled at how such a heavy, massive door could be held closed by two such small pieces of metal. The door could only be opened if I rose from my chair, went over to it, and turned the handle. If someone were to knock on the door it would be my choice how to respond; I could either open the door, if that were convenient for me, or I could ask the person knocking to wait, or I could even ignore the knocking altogether if I was doing something particularly interesting and important.

I went on to remark on how safe and secure it made me feel to know that no one could come through my door unless I chose to open it; I had the control. As I spoke, Trevor gazed at the two prongs in the door edge, and I suggested he make a picture of them holding the door securely shut. Whenever he felt the urge to go to the bathroom, that picture would remind him and reassure him that he could keep his little muscles closed and comfortable until he was free to go to the bathroom.

This simple suggestion was followed by a marked decrease in the frequency of Trevor's accidents. Several weeks later, however, while sitting on the floor of the therapy room engaged in play with a dolls' house, Trevor suddenly stopped and, in an urgent voice, asked to go to the bathroom. I mentioned that our time together would soon be over and asked him to wait. He squirmed and said that he couldn't wait, pleading to go. I then reminded him of my door and its two small but very strong bolts, that held it securely shut and reminded him of his stomach which could work in the same way.

I glanced down and noticed that although Trevor had started to wet, he had now stopped himself. The urine stain was small. I commented on this, congratulating him on his self-control, and I pointed out that although he had started to wet, once he remembered his muscles, he was able to stop. As I continued talking, the muscle tension in his face lessened and he resumed his play. I again compared his sensation of having to go to the bathroom to knocks on my door. To concretize this still further, I had him stand on one side of my door while I stood on the other and knocked. I told him that he could open it if and whenever he wished, but that he had the control.

Trevor allowed me to knock loudly for some time and then finally opened the door. I repeated the exercise once more but this time, after knocking loudly at first, I diminished the volume and intensity until it became very faint. At that point he again opened the door and together we observed that, although my knocking began loudly, when he ignored it it gradually diminished to the point of almost disappearing. Again, we compared this with Trevor's bodily sensations which at first can be very strong, but will gradually become weaker and weaker, and may disappear entirely if he chooses to ignore them by busying himself with something else.

Trevor seemed intrigued by the above exercise and left the session with a buoyancy and confidence not previously evident. In the following weeks the incidence of his daytime wetting decreased further until he became completely dry.

In this approach to the treatment of daytime wetting several metaphorical devices were used. The door and the tiny pieces of metal that keep it shut are metaphorical objects. By analogy, Trevor is asked to compare the door and its two small pieces of metal with his own muscles. Trevor is given the metaphorical task of standing at the door and waiting while someone knocks. Finally, an artistic metaphor is used when Trevor is asked to make a picture of the two prongs holding the door shut.

Similar metaphors can be useful in the treatment of some cases of encopresis, principally those in which there are emotional factors that have resulted in the child becoming resigned to being unable to control bowel function. Soiling that is not due to organic disease or chronic constipation may, however, belong to one of several categories. It may be due, for example, to failure of the parents or parent-substitutes to provide appropriate and consistent toilet training. Or it may be "regressive"; that is, part of the process of regressing to an earlier developmental stage by which some children (and adults) react to certain stresses. Or it may be "aggressive"; that is, a somewhat (but not very) indirect way of expressing angry feelings, often toward parents. (These categories are discussed further in Barker, 1983, Chapter 7.) Sometimes more than one of these processes may be operating, and other emotional and family systems factors may also contribute to the maintenance of the symptom. The combination of enuresis and encopresis is not unusual, though it is more common for soilers also to wet themselves than for enuretics to have the additional problem of soiling.

When children have received inadequate toilet training, other family problems often need to be dealt with. Indeed, Anthony (1957) describes the families of these children as having massive problems and as generally functioning poorly, being burdened with many problems in addition to their wet and dirty children. The other problems, or some of them, may need to be dealt with first, and metaphors may not be needed as a part of the therapy plan. If metaphors about training are to be used however, stories about the training of athletes, circus animals and household pets may be used. (The story of Rosalie's dog, mentioned in Chapter 8, could be modified for use in this context.) And there are many examples of people—musicians, artists, craftsmen of various sorts—who have achieved their ambitions and success only through hard, conscientious practice.

When fecal soiling represents the expression of aggressive feelings, metaphors about how aggression may be turned to constructive use may be helpful. The biblical example of Saint Paul, describing his behavior both before and after his conversion, appeals to some. Before Paul's conversion he was aggressively active in persecuting Christians, but after he became converted to Christianity he was one of the most active, fearless, and aggressive preachers of the gospel. Stories also abound about angry

young men becoming successful businessmen, and violent crimi-
nals reforming their lives and energetically turning their aggressive drives to good works. Metaphors about powerful machines
that can either function well and contribute constructively to society or be used for destructive purposes may also be useful. The
ultimate example here, perhaps, is nuclear power.

Metaphors useful in treating children with regressive soiling
tend to be similar in principle, though not necessarily in content,
to those used for developmental reframing, as discussed in Chapter 5. That is, they present the symptom as behavior that is normal but appropriate for a younger age group. Stories about people modifying their behavior as they mature may therefore be
useful metaphors.

ADDICTIONS

Most clients seeking help in overcoming alcohol and drug
abuse and other addictions have, as we have said, a basic problem of low self-esteem. Ways of helping people increase their self-
esteem have already been discussed, but metaphors may be useful also in dealing with other aspects of these clients' problems.
Precisely how metaphorical methods are used will depend on
therapists' understanding of the dynamics of substance abuse
generally, their assessment of the particular client or family under
treatment, and their philosophy of change—that is, how they
believe change can be facilitated in these cases. The following are
some of the issues that may need to be addressed in the treatment of these clients.

The experience of being "high" or "loaded."   In Chapter 1, it was
suggested that the mythological tale of Daedalus and Icarus could
be used as a warning against getting too "high," since this was
the cause of Icarus' downfall and death. But getting high is construed as a pleasant experience by those who use drugs of addiction; thus it may be helpful to suggest that there are other,
less dangerous ways of getting "high."

I sometimes tell patients who have problems of substance

abuse about a woman in her late twenties with whom I used hypnotherapy to treat various problems. When in her teens and early twenties this woman had been seriously involved in the use of street drugs and alcohol, and as a result her children had been taken into foster care. Subsequently the young woman underwent treatment, and she had now been off drugs and alcohol for several years. Moreover, her children had been returned to her. She observed, after coming out of trance one day, "If only you could bottle up that stuff and sell it, you would make a fortune. It's almost as good as getting high on cocaine."

This story can be told by way of explaining what hypnosis is, something that may need to be discussed when hypnotherapy is suggested. But it also carries a message that there are other ways of getting to feel good about oneself, and indeed that the necessary resources are there within oneself, available without any use of chemicals. Similar points can be made by telling about people who have become "addicted" to hobbies, sports, marathon running, music, and other activities that are less harmful than drugs.

The social associations of drug and alcohol use.   Drug and alcohol use is usually a group activity. Although many substance abusers become quite withdrawn from others, most have been introduced to the drugs they use by others, and an important part of their basic motivation is a desire to be a part of the group. Leaving one group of friends—those in whose company the person has been abusing drugs—for another one, in which drugs are not abused (which may or may not be a group of recovered drug abusers), may therefore be helpful to those striving to overcome addictive behavior. Moreover, many drug and alcohol abusers are socially isolated, their use of drugs being part of an attempt to make social relationships; so helping them to make such relationships in other ways may also be therapeutically helpful. In assisting clients to make such changes (which it is usually not easy to do), metaphors can be more effective than direct injunctions.

Reframing the drug use and offering alternatives.   Discussing the role of drugs as behavior reinforcers, Blum (1984) writes:

Drug dependence should be approached with the understanding that there are multiple causative and contributing
factors. The more one understands this, the more one ap-
preciates the awesome complexities of this disorder—if one
accepts it as a disorder. One should realize that the contemporary hard-core criminal addicts are far more products of
societal actions than of their basic personalities or of the
pharmacology of heroin. Certainly treatment programs . . .
should direct their efforts to improving the quality of life,
providing meaningful options while facilitating change, and
giving individuals a choice in deciding what they will do
with the rest of their lives. (p. 7)

How may we use metaphor to achieve the therapeutic aims
Blum recommends in the above quotation? Greek mythology offers us the story of Pandora's box, which contains some relevant
metaphors.

Soon after the world was created, when there were no
women, only men, in the world, the gods Zeus and Prometheus quarreled. Zeus didn't want men to have fire, so he
hid it away, but Prometheus found it and gave it to mankind. This made Zeus very angry and he decided to cause
trouble to men.
Zeus proceeded to make a woman and he called her Pandora, which means "all-gifted." Athena, the goddess of
wisdom and handicrafts, gave her silken garments, a heavy
gold chain for her waist and flowers for her hair, and she
also taught her needlework and housecraft. Hermes, the
messenger of the gods, taught her how to get her way with
men by clever lies and crafty words. Aphrodite, goddess of
love and beauty, made her so beautiful that she would be
desired by all men, but she also put cruel longings and cares
into Pandora's heart. Zeus then breathed life into Pandora.
Zeus' gift to Pandora was a heavy, jewel-encrusted box,
which he warned her she must never open. He then told Hermes to take Pandora to Prometheus's brother, Epimetheus.
Prometheus, who was undergoing punishment for giving
fire to men, warned Epimetheus not to accept any gift from
Zeus. The headstrong and impulsive Epimetheus, however,

instantly fell in love with Pandora. Hermes told him he was
the most fortunate of men, for Zeus had given him the first
woman to be his bride and mother of his children. Epimetheus gladly accepted Pandora and she became his wife.

At first Epimetheus was very happy with his wife, who
was both talented and beautiful; but she brought sorrow as
well as joy. She teased her husband and made him jealous,
and caused him cares and worries he never had before. She
also thought more and more about that box. What priceless
gifts from the gods might it contain? She begged Epimetheus
to let her open it, but he told her not to do so because this
would be against the wishes of the mighty gods.

Temptation eventually became too much for Pandora.
One day, when Epimetheus was out, she said to herself,
"No one will ever know if I take a peep into the box." She
went to the far corner of the house where the box was stored.
She found the lid heavy and hard to raise, but after a while
she managed to pry it open. While it was still only slightly
lifted from the box, there was a great noise, like fluttering
wings, and out flew all the many troubles that now plague
mankind: pain, decay, old age, want, worry, toil, hunger,
envy, revenge and hatred, along with all the diseases that
cause sickness and death.

Pandora tried to close the lid as quickly as she could but
it was too late! In those few seconds she had released into
the world all the evils and sorrows we now experience. But
one good thing did come out of the box. Zeus had been
thoughtful enough to include in the box, hope—something
which also rests in every human heart and can, if used rightly, overcome all the evils that preceded it out of the box.

This tale is rich in symbolism. Pandora, artificially created by
Zeus as a punishment for mankind, seems to me a rather nice
metaphor for euphoriant drugs—beautiful, much to be desired,
but in the end cruel and destructive and bringing unhappiness.
The box, too, could represent drugs of addiction. Once you start
them, it is hard to go back, just as Pandora couldn't quickly close
the box again; the damage had been done.

Perhaps Pandora should represent drugs themselves, which

bring first joy, then sorrow, and the box should represent their evil properties, which are many and can only be overcome with hope. This mythological story also makes other points: for example, what is forbidden is often especially attractive, and if you do not obey society's (or the gods') rules unfortunate things will happen to you.

Of course, it is not the therapist who decides what Pandora, or the box, might represent, but the client's unconscious mind. Our clients may not use the metaphors we offer them in the ways we suggest, intend, or hope. It is nevertheless important that we plan our metaphorical interventions carefully. A therapeutically useful message should be offered, even if it is not accepted; and if the metaphorical messages we offer are repeatedly ignored or rejected, we should reconsider our diagnostic assessment.

Telling this story, or others making similar points, is unlikely in itself to cure any drug addicts. But such metaphors do have the potential to be useful as parts of more comprehensive, perhaps long-term, therapeutic plans. It may be necessary to use many metaphors, as well as other strategic devices, in the course of treatment, and to embed them in other material, as will be described in Chapter 11. Nevertheless, stories like that of Pandora's box may contribute to the reframing of clients' problems, and may promote gradual change in clients' views of their situations.

ENTERING THE PSYCHOTIC WORLD THROUGH THE USE OF METAPHOR

The psychotherapy of psychotic disorders is a complex and specialized process that we cannot deal with here in depth. The role of metaphor in the treatment of psychoses is not well established, but the following clinical example is offered to illustrate one possible way in which metaphorical methods may be of value.

Yvette was 12. She was said always to have been shy and quiet, and she had few friends. She was referred for psychiatric assessment at the suggestion of her teacher at school, where Yvette was in a special class. Yvette's academic progress was poor, she had become almost completely socially isolated, and her behavior was becoming increasingly bizarre.

Because of diagnostic uncertainty, Yvette was admitted to a children's psychiatric inpatient unit for assessment. It became clear that she was auditorily hallucinated and also held a number of delusional beliefs. A diagnosis of juvenile schizophrenia was made.

Assessment of the family indicated that the relationship between Yvette and her mother was a closely enmeshed one, and that there was much emotional distance between Yvette and her 10-year-old sister Zoe. The father seemed to play little part in Yvette's life, though he agreed passively with his wife's views about Yvette. Yvette's mother treated her as a very special child who required much care and who could not be expected to do most of the things a normal 12-year-old would do. It seemed, though, that Yvette was getting conflicting messages about whether or not she should grow up and become more independent of the parents; they said she should but demanded little of her and accepted her quiet, withdrawn ways as just the way she was and—probably, they seemed to think—the way she always would be.

Family therapy was recommended, and the parents agreed to this. Progress was at first slow; the parents, led by the mother, seemed reluctant to accept that there was anything very much wrong with Yvette. Yes, she was quiet, they agreed, and she didn't have many friends, but this was just the kind of person she was. The parents were particularly upset by the suggestion that Yvette was hallucinated. It was true, they admitted, that she had some "imaginary friends" to whom she spoke and who spoke to her. She also talked with her mother about these people but, the parents insisted, this was not unusual—lots of children had imaginary friends, and Yvette's had just stayed around a little longer than most other children's.

In view of the family's reluctance to accept that Yvette was either hallucinated or deluded, the therapist, and his team of observing colleagues, decided to accept the family's view of things. The team therefore agreed that Yvette had imaginary friends with whom she talked and who were, in certain ways, a help and a comfort to her. While perhaps she was rather old to have so many imaginary friends, or even to have any, she had always been a quiet, shy girl with few real friends; so it was understandable that she had not yet been able to abandon her imaginary ones. The clinical situation was thus reframed in developmental terms; Yvette was not crazy, she was just late giving up imaginary friends.

Once the above view of Yvette's symptoms had been agreed with the family, a mass of information about Yvette's delusional world emerged. It was rather like a complex, long-running soap opera, with some characters coming and going while others remained constantly present; people got married and divorced, had children, got killed, lost their jobs, and so on. The therapy team was also interested to discover that the mother seemed to know almost as much about the "soap opera" as Yvette, and certainly more than anyone else in the family.

While the parents had been reluctant to accept that Yvette was hallucinated or psychotic, they found it impossible to deny that it would be better for her to have more real friends and fewer imaginary ones. Achieving this therefore became an agreed aim of treatment. The family appeared now to be engaged in therapy; rapport was established and some therapeutic goals had been agreed. Having a need for "imaginary friends," and communicating with these people, had become a metaphor for the psychotic process.

After the above understanding had been reached, therapy was able to proceed in a spirit of cooperation between family and therapist. There were signs that Yvette was beginning to make some friends in her special class at school, and it was suggested that, as her circle of real-life friends widened she would have less and less need for imaginary ones.

A program was now developed whereby Yvette was allowed to talk out loud to her imaginary friends only at certain times; the times when she could discuss them with her mother, or other family members, were also restricted. These regulations were presented as being in part a response to Yvette's gradual acquisition of friends at school, and in part a way of encouraging her to make yet more friends, while at the same time she was not totally deprived of the comfort of the "imaginary" ones. This process was continued until Yvette could talk with her friends, or discuss them with anyone, only on Saturdays—the situation that exists as this is written.

In treating Yvette's family there were many issues that had to be dealt with in what was a complex clinical problem. The above account, which has concentrated on one aspect of the therapy, is intended to make the point that symptoms can themselves be represented metaphorically. This can be helpful when a family or a client refuse to accept the treating professional's view of certain symptomatic behavior; in a sense the parents themselves were involved in the psychotic process. The process of having imaginary friends and then giving them up for real ones became a metaphor for being in a psychotic, delusional world and coming out of it.

Treating psychotic behavior by initially accepting clients' delusional beliefs and then reframing them metaphorically (as when Yvette's symptoms were reframed in developmental terms) may be a therapeutic approach that holds promise. The therapist who wishes to treat a psychotic person using psychotherapy should first obtain a clear mental picture of the client's delusional world. It may then be possible to create a metaphor for the psychotic situation that can be used therapeutically.

TERMINATION METAPHORS

It is sometimes helpful, when therapy sessions end, to leave clients with resources they can continue to use, even though they are no longer under treatment. This procedure serves a function similar to that of tasks prescribed to be carried out between sessions; such tasks can keep clients and therapist involved, and they can often help clients to continue to change in the therapist's absence. The resources used when therapy ends may be objects, activities, rituals—even just words or phrases. These "termination devices," however, usually have a metaphorical meaning.

An example of the use of a metaphorical object in this way has been mentioned in Chapter 5. In that case a mother tended needlessly to treat her daughter with "kid gloves." The mother and daughter were instructed to freeze a pair of kid gloves, and the mother was told that if, at any time in the future, she felt she should still treat her daughter "with kid gloves" she could do so, but only after removing the gloves from the freezer and thawing them out. This of course would cause the mother to delay instituting the behavior she was considering, and it would also make both mother and child think about the situation and consider whether treatment "with kid gloves" was really needed. It also turned out to be a source of merriment and laughter and became part of the family's "private language."

Coppersmith (in press) has described yet another example of the creative use of metaphorical objects as part of a termination ritual. These objects were offered at the end of the treatment of a family in which the 12-year-old daughter had had an eating problem. Among the very few foods the daughter would eat were french fried potatoes. She was seeing a dietician who urged her to eat various other foods, notably kiwi fruit, which she hated.

At the final therapy session the therapist handed the family a potato and a kiwi fruit, and instructed them to put these items in a plastic bowl, fill the bowl with water, and place it at the back of their freezer. When, in the future, the family found themselves in a quandary regarding what to do about a problem within the family, they were to remove the bowl from the freezer, allow the contents to thaw out, and have a family discussion about the seriousness of the problem and about the course of action they should take. The potato and the kiwi fruit of course symbolized the process the family had been through in solving the problem for which they had come to therapy. The pair of objects might be said to be an "anchor" for the family's problem-solving resources.

SUMMARY

Metaphors may be of use in the psychotherapy of a wide variety of conditions in addition to those dealt with in earlier chapters. Any information that needs to be communicated as part of a therapeutic plan may be communicated metaphorically, rather than directly, if this is indicated.

Metaphors may be used to bring about an increase in self-esteem, by suggesting that individuals' fixed ideas about themselves may not be valid, and that they have strengths, resources

and personality assets of which they have been unaware. Metaphors may be used in the treatment of enuretic and encopretic
children, who may be shown that they too have hitherto unrecognized abilities, namely ways of using their muscles and other
resources to control their bladders and bowels. Metaphors may
be useful in dealing with problems of addiction and drug abuse,
by suggesting alternative ways of achieving what people have
been trying to achieve through the use of drugs. Finally, it is
possible to enter the psychotic world by treating psychotic symptoms metaphorically, so that they become real-life issues, which
therapy can then address.

Metaphorical devices, which may be objects, tasks, or rituals,
can also be used when therapy is terminated, in order to provide
clients with resources they can continue to use. These devices
are usually metaphors for some aspect of what has happened in
therapy, or of the changes the clients have made during treatment.

TWO PRACTICAL EXERCISES

*1) In the foregoing section on the social associations of drug and alcohol
use, it was suggested that clients can sometimes benefit as a result of
changing their friends and social circles, so that they have less contact
with drug and alcohol users. Devise a metaphorical way of putting this
point across.*
*2) Suggest two possible termination metaphors for use in the case of
Rosalie's dog, described in Chapter 6.*

11

The Practical Delivery of Metaphors

CLEANING CARPETS

A new and highly efficient carpet cleaning system became available. Two companies bought it, and each set about marketing it in the same city. Their equipment was identical and their staffs were equally well-trained and competent.

The sales manager of the first firm, ABC Carpet Cleaners, decided to use telephone soliciting to sell the service. So he hired a number of young, unemployed men and women to call up lists of people and invite them to have their carpets cleaned by this revolutionary new process. He paid the minimum wage, plus a small commission on sales. As his staff had little experience of selling things, he prepared a script for them, one that moved quite quickly to the key question, "Do you want your carpets cleaned by a revolutionary new method, at about two-thirds of what you would pay for a regular carpet cleaning service?"

This offer sounded like a pretty good deal, the sales manager thought, but the response to the telephone calls was disappointing. Many people hung up as soon as they realized the caller was a salesperson, and others when they heard mention of the term "carpet cleaning." The reactions of the men and women who were making the calls were also disappointing. Many quickly became disillusioned with the job and resigned even though, for most of them, the only likely alternative was unemployment. They felt they were selling a good service, but they also felt that they could not really make contact with the people they called.

The sales manager of the other company, XYZ Cleaning Systems, had a different approach. He rented space for a week or two in a number of busy shopping malls. In each mall he set up a small enclosure with a few comfortable chairs, free coffee and tea, and information about carpet cleaning that focused particularly on the method his firm was offering as an improvement on "old fashioned systems." The sales staff had available a short videotape presentation, showing a carpet being cleaned, with "before and after" pictures of carpets.

The salespeople were personable young men and women, attractively dressed, who had been selected on the basis of their ability to engage customers in conversation and make them feel at home. They were instructed to invite passers-by into the enclosure for coffee or tea. They were then to engage them in conversation on whatever seemed to interest them. Carpet cleaning was only to be mentioned by the staff once they felt they were getting along well with their potential customers.

This approach was more expensive than the first-mentioned one. Renting the space was costly, the sales staff were better paid, time had to be spent training them, and a far more detailed manual was prepared for their use than the brief script given to ABC's telephone solicitors. Although a great deal more time was spent with each prospect, the time, trouble, and expense paid off; XYZ Cleaning Systems got more business than did ABC Carpet Cleaners.

Eventually ABC Carpet Cleaners declared bankruptcy, while XYZ Cleaning Systems flourished and became a highly successful company.

ESTABLISHING RAPPORT

Whatever form of psychotherapy is being employed it is important for therapists to establish a good rapport with their clients. The importance of rapport does, however, seem to vary according to the type of therapy being carried out. In strategic therapy—and metaphor is usually employed as part of a strategic plan—rapport generally needs to be strong, because clients are often assigned tasks that may not have much obvious relevance to the problems for which they have come for help. Carrying out unusual assignments, or listening to stories from Greek mythology or the world of computers, for example, are not what most of our clients expect, at least when they first come to us. The strategic therapist takes responsibility for helping clients make the changes they seek, and develops for each of them a plan designed to achieve this aim; however, this plan is not usually explained to the clients. Moreover, it involves some form of indirect approach to achieving the therapeutic goals.

Indirect forms of therapy require a trusting relationship between client and therapist, and trust tends to develop with rapport. Trust is not quite the same as rapport; for trust to develop, it is helpful for the client not only to be in a state of deep rapport with the therapist, but also to believe that the therapist is a competent professional. Such beliefs arise from the therapist's reputation in the community, the experience the client understands the therapist to have had of the kind of problems he or she faces, and so on, as well as from the actual process of the interviews and the way therapy is conducted. Unless clients have a deeply trusting relationship with their therapist, they may reject what the therapist says to them and fail to carry out assigned tasks; indeed they may drop out of treatment altogether.

Hypnotherapists have long recognized the vital roles of rapport and trust. They know that failure to induce trance usually means that these features of the therapeutic relationship—rapport and trust—are present to an insufficient degree. Rather than dubbing their clients "resistant," they prefer to define the problem as a lack of sufficient trust and a need to increase the level of rapport that exists between them and the clients concerned. In other forms of psychotherapy, too, failure is often due to a lack of rapport, also referred to as a failure of engagement.

What is rapport? To be in rapport with a person implies that there exists a sympathetic relationship and a state of understanding, harmony, and accord. The understanding, of course will be less than total, but it can be expected to increase as the relationship develops and rapport increases. Another aspect of rapport is an intense involvement between the persons concerned. Erickson, Hershman and Sector (1961), in their book on medical and dental hypnosis, describe rapport as

> that peculiar relationship, existing between subject and operator, wherein, since it [hypnosis] is a cooperative endeavor, the subject's attention is directed to the operator, and the operator's attention is directed to the subject. Hence, the subject tends to pay no attention to externals or the environmental situation. . . . (p. 66)

Rapport is hard to define precisely in words, but it is relatively easy to recognize in practice. When it is well developed the therapist can say almost anything, however outrageous, to the client without the latter becoming upset; if the remark is one that could be construed as insulting, the client will regard it as a joke, or at least as something that is not meant seriously. When rapport is established, the client is intensely involved with, trusts, and feels warmly towards the therapist, and generally has positive expectations of the therapeutic process.

When rapport is profound enough, metaphors that may, to the conscious mind, seem silly and quite unrelated to the objectives of therapy are easily accepted. This is important, for the whole point of metaphors is that they do appear to be off topic, despite having relevant metaphorical meanings.

What follows in this section will be somewhat redundant for those experienced therapists who regularly use the techniques discussed. It will be important, however, for those who may not be making full use of these techniques, since those who do not take the time and trouble to establish adequate rapport are likely to have their metaphors—and other interventions—rejected or ignored by their clients, both consciously and unconsciously. (Rapport is of course important in social interactions of any sort, not just psychotherapeutic ones, but we will confine our discussion to therapy. Bear in mind, however, that the techniques to be described below have wide application; they can be useful in dealing with students, salespersons, customers, clients in fields other than therapy, friends, enemies, colleagues, bosses, subordinates, relatives—indeed anyone with whom one wants to relate effectively.)

The promotion of rapport requires the use of both nonverbal and verbal techniques, but the nonverbal ones are the more important. Virtually everything therapists do and say, including their intonation and way of speaking, has its effect, positive or negative, on the development of rapport.

Nonverbal Rapport-Building Techniques

The nonverbal messages a therapist sends to a client start at the first meeting, perhaps even before this if there is a telephone contact or communication by letter. A warm, friendly tone of voice, and the use, in a sincere way, of courtesies like "Good morning," "It was good of you to wait while I was speaking to a colleague," or "I'm sorry I wasn't able to call you back yesterday," get the relationship off to a good start. It helps if the therapist goes to meet the clients where they are waiting to greet them, rather than have them ushered into the office or therapy room by someone else. The manner in which clients are greeted is important too; it should be matched to their social style and should convey respect, warmth, interest, acceptance, and optimism.

Having available a suitably furnished and equipped room helps establish rapport. Ideally the office or therapy room should have comfortable chairs for therapist and clients, there should not be a desk or other large item of furniture between therapist and clients—though a low coffee table may be acceptable—and the room should be well ventilated, temperature-controlled, and lit in a way that is neither glaringly bright nor gloomily dark. Younger children are usually best seen in a playroom, or at least a room containing toys, play materials and drawing or painting equipment appropriate to their age.

Useful as it is to have a suitable room in which to see clients, the most important factor by far is the behavior of the therapist; it is perfectly possible to establish good rapport with people in prison cells, restaurants, or school classrooms or sitting beside a swimming pool or on the beach—indeed, just about anywhere one may need or choose to conduct interviews.

The therapist's mode of dress carries its own message. Clients generally expect their therapist to be cleanly and respectably dressed and well groomed. White coats, which doctors sometimes wear in hospitals, tend to intimidate children and adults alike and are probably best avoided. But dress, too, is less important than the therapist's behavior.

The behavior that most effectively promotes rapport matches the client's behavior. That is, it is useful to match the client's body posture and movements, rate of breathing, speed of talking, and voice tone. These techniques are familiar to hypnotherapists who, for example, commonly time their spoken phrases to pace their clients' breathing. It can be effective also to "cross-match" clients' behavior; if, for example, a client is rhythmically moving a foot or hand in a particular way the therapist might match this by tapping a pencil with the same rhythm. It is not necessary to match all features of a client's behavior and the matching should be done sensitively and unobtrusively. Crossing and uncrossing the legs, the tilt of the head and whether the client is leaning forward or relaxing against the back of the chair are examples of features of clients' behavior that it can be helpful to match.

These devices are all aspects of what Dilts and his colleagues (1980) call "pacing." They explain the process as follows:

> When you pace someone—by communicating from the context of their model of the world—you become synchronized with their own internal processes. It is, in one sense, an explicit means to "second guess" people or to "read their minds," because you know how they will respond to your communications. This kind of synchrony can serve to reduce resistance between you and the people with whom you are communicating. The strongest form of synchrony is the con-

tinuous presentation of your communication in sequences which perfectly parallel the unconscious processes of the person you are communicating with—such communication approaches the much desired goal of irresistibility. (Dilts et al., 1980, pp. 116–7)

Verbal Rapport-Building Techniques

The therapist's verbal communications can also assist or impede the development of rapport. The developers of neurolinguistic programming have pointed out that rapport is promoted by matching the predicates used by the person with whom one wishes to establish rapport (Bandler, Grinder, & Satir, 1976; Bandler & Grinder, 1979). Predicates are the words that describe the way things are and include verbs, adjectives, and adverbs. Thus if the client favors visual predicates in describing things ("I see what you're getting at," "Things are looking brighter," "It all seems pretty hazy to me," and so on), the therapist should respond with similar predicates in order to gain rapport. If a client uses mainly auditory predicates ("I hear what you're saying," "Things sound bad to me," "It was like music to my ears"), the therapist should respond accordingly. "Kinesthetic" or feeling-type expressions ("That was a weight off my shoulders," "Somehow that doesn't feel right," "I felt my heart skip a beat") should be matched with responses couched in feeling-type terms.

These verbal techniques are effective for reasons similar to those that explain the effectiveness of the nonverbal techniques. They work because, like the nonverbal techniques, they create a synchrony between the communications offered by the therapist and the internal processes of the client—as Dilts et al. (1980) explain in the passage quoted earlier.

It is worthwhile listening carefully to what your clients say and how they express themselves, not only in order to match their predicates, but also so that you can gain a knowledge of the vocabulary with which they are familiar. This is especially important with children, but it applies to adults also. The vocabulary of a university professor is likely to be more extensive than that of a laborer with a Grade 9 education, and a conscious effort to match each one's use of language repays the effort in increased rapport. There are few things that impede the establishment of rapport as much as repeatedly using words that clients do not understand. Those who work with children quickly learn the necessity of always bearing in mind, and taking into account, their clients' vocabulary and language skills.

While rapport is being established it is usually best to accept a client's view of things. Clients sometimes express various un-justified fears, worries, depressive thoughts, or obsessional ideas; they may also voice beliefs and espouse values with which a therapist disagrees, perhaps strongly. There may come a time when it is appropriate to challenge these ideas, but they should usually be accepted until rapport is well established.

Milton Erickson, who was highly skilled both as a hypnothera-pist and as an interviewer, had a way of accepting his patients' statements while at the same time adding something significant to them. Thus if a patient came to him and said she was feeling deeply depressed, had no future, and had been thinking of kill-ing herself, he might say to her, ''So you've been feeling very low, you're depressed, you have little hope for the future and you've even been thinking about killing yourself, *and you really don't know how much longer you're going to feel this way, or when the depression will lift.''*

In such an interaction the therapist has denied nothing the pa-tient has said, but has added a tag on the end of his reply which it is hard for the patient to deny; it is indeed true that she does not know when her depression will lift, but the statement by the therapist also contains the embedded message that at some time in the future it *will* lift.

It is possible to carry the above process further and discuss possible time frames for the lifting of the depression, for exam-ple by saying something like, ''You don't know whether it's go-ing to last another week, or two weeks, or perhaps even as much as a whole month.'' This is better than saying, ''Cheer up you'll soon feel better,'' a remark that is likely to irritate a depressed person. The former statement offers the prospect of recovery from the depression, and suggests a time frame, without directly challenging the patient's view of herself. This type of statement is not always appropriate, of course, but the approach offers a way of promoting rapport while also helping the subject to regain some hope or to see things from a different perspective.

The last rapport-building technique we will discuss here consists of adopting the "one-down" position with clients. Invariably there are things about which clients know more than their therapists, and it can be useful to ask clients to help by giving the correct spelling of their names, explaining what their job involves, or describing their town or part of the country or, if they are immigrants, the country from which they come. Sometimes therapists will find that clients have particular things in common with them; perhaps they come from the same place or have an interest in the same hobby or sport. In that case therapists might comment on this and perhaps exchange a few words on these shared experiences or interests.

DELIVERING METAPHORS

A real estate agent once told me that there are three important things in determining how readily a house sells and for what price. The first is location; the second is location; and the third is—yes, you've guessed it—location. In other words context is everything, or nearly everything. Much the same applies to delivering metaphors.

The right context for delivering metaphors is one in which, from the start, stories are told, tasks are given, and points are illustrated by the use of similes and analogies. This sets the tone of the sessions and defines them as occasions on which stories and the like are to be expected. Clients are not then surprised when further stories are told or tasks set, though these latter ones may be intended as therapeutic metaphors and part of a strategic therapy plan. Therapists who wish to use metaphors, therefore, must construct contexts in which stories and activities are the norm. Their clients will quickly come to expect these things. Major therapeutic metaphors are likely to be ineffective if they are introduced out of the blue because the therapist has suddenly thought of this new device, or because it has been recommended by a colleague or supervisor (or because he or she has been inspired to use it by reading this book!). Tasks intended to have metaphorical meanings may be more readily carried out if there have been other tasks of more obvious relevance assigned and carried out previously.

Introducing the metaphorical story or task and getting clients' attention and compliance are usually easy if the foregoing conditions have been met. Nevertheless, there are certain ways of offering clients stories and tasks that help to secure acceptance. Anecdotes, analogies, and brief metaphorical allusions, on the other hand, are generally accepted without much question; for example, it would probably be quite easy to use the following anecdote to make a point to parents.

> [This reminds me of Jane Austen and her mother.] Did you know that Jane's mother was always telling her that her scribbling would ruin her eyesight? It seems she didn't approve of her daughter's writing. Now I understand there's Jane Austen fever in North America. What a good thing it was that Jane continued writing despite the alleged risk to her eyesight!

This anecdote might be delivered with or without the sentence in square brackets, but either way the "metaphorical disguise" of the message is quite thin. In other words, most families to whom this anecdote is told will probably realize at once why the therapist is telling it, and will recognize its message. This does not mean that the anecdote will be ineffective; addressed to someone who loves the works of Jane Austen it might be a powerful way of making the points that parents sometimes need to let their offspring do their own thing, that they do not always recognize their children's talents and that their advice is not invariably right. Others might first need to be told who Jane Austen was and why her books are so well regarded.

The repeated use of anecdotes such as this one prepares clients for longer metaphors with deeper meanings. Longer stories without intended deep metaphorical meanings may be used for the same purpose. Another device is to tell stories or anecdotes about other clients; because such stories concern psychotherapy, clients more readily assume that they have some relevance. As has been mentioned in Chapter 5, this can be a double-edged weapon; hearing others' histories recounted could make clients fear that their own case histories will be discussed with other clients. There are various ways of avoiding this danger. One is to set the case being discussed in another location, preferably a different country, or at least a different province or state. Another is to introduce such material very casually saying, for example, ''A client (or a family) I once saw . . . ,'' or ''I once heard about some people who went to a therapist. . . . '' In any event it is important always to be careful to imply and, when necessary, state that you take confidentiality seriously and will not breach your clients' confidences. Where a good level of rapport and trust exist, however, this is naturally assumed by clients, and difficulties are most unlikely to arise.

Provided that rapport has been well developed and that a context has been created in which storytelling and related activities are the norm, it is not usually necessary to do much more than tell the story or assign the task. There are, however, some introductory phrases that can be useful. These include, ''You might be interested in . . . ,'' ''I've found that some families are intrigued by an experience I had when I was in . . . ,'' and ''I wonder what you will make of this . . . '' When a task is to be assigned it may be introduced by saying, ''An experiment that might be fun for you is . . . ,'' or ''I'd be very interested to see what happens when you try this at home . . . ''

These phrases and others like them carry messages that may arouse clients' interest or curiosity, preferably both. Note that they are all permissive, rather than injunctive. They do not tell clients they *must* listen to what is being told them, or carry out the tasks suggested; they suggest rather that the clients might get something worthwhile or interesting out of what is proposed by the therapist, or at least it might be fun. It is then up to the therapist to ensure that what happens is interesting, or fun, or whatever has been suggested. Some of the foregoing phrases also imply that the therapist may gain something of value from observing the response of the clients to the story or task. Given the right client–therapist relationship, in which rapport is well developed, this may be a motivating factor.

TELLING STORIES

There is a great deal to the telling of stories, and most of us can readily distinguish between a good storyteller and a poor one. Some general principles are as follows:

- Be prepared with your story before you start; as with most activities, careful preparation pays dividends.
- Take your time, don't rush things, and vary your pace and style of delivery.
- Pay careful attention to what needs to be emphasized; included in the content of stories used as therapeutic metaphors will be key phrases or passages, and you should mark these out by slowing your delivery, or altering your voice tone or pitch, or by some other device that distinguishes these sections.
- Make the story sound interesting; this is easier if you find the story interesting yourself; it may be wise to avoid stories that you find boring.
- Pay careful attention to the responses, especially the nonverbal ones, of your listeners, modifying your technique accordingly.

The nonverbal messages offered when a story is told are of course very important. Good storytellers use gestures, pantomime, facial expressions, laughter, variations of voice, and other nonverbal devices to tell much of the story. It is not so much the story's manifest content, expressed in "digital" language (Watzlawick et al., 1967) that is important; indeed the story's impact on the right brain may depend much more on the nonverbal than the verbal material the teller offers.

TIMING OF THERAPEUTIC METAPHORS

Anecdotes, similes, and analogies are common conversational devices that may be slipped into the conversation at any time. Therapists who plan to make regular use of other forms of metaphor, however, should set the stage for this early on by the frequent use of stories, tasks, or whatever other devices they prefer to employ.

Much the same applies to relationship metaphors, although these are sometimes ongoing processes rather than discrete interventions offered at particular times. Thus if there is a problem in the relationship between father and son in a family group, the relationship between therapist and father may become a metaphor for that between father and son. This is sometimes referred to as "modeling," but there can be much more to this process than simply showing the father how he should relate to his son; indeed, the process of modeling is often better done by the therapist interacting directly with the son. But when parents have lacked proper care, love, and security as children, it may be hard for them to provide these things for their own children. In that case it may help them to be cared for, and shown love, true concern, and a confidence in their ability to live successful lives, by the therapist. This relationship can then become, over time, a metaphor for that between parent and child. This process, which can be therapeutically very helpful, will often be a long-term one, perhaps extending over a period of months, or even longer.

Major metaphorical stories are often best offered at, or near, the end of a session. Occasionally it works out well if they are presented as "time-fillers"; that is, they may be introduced with a phrase such as, "I see we have some time left before the session is due to end, so perhaps you would like to hear about . . . " This can be a helpful approach with clients who have a negative attitude toward this type of intervention. It is then the responsibility of the therapist to engage the clients' attention and interest. On the other hand, this approach also tends to play down the importance of what is about to be said or suggested. When satisfactory rapport exists between therapist and clients, it is usually unnecessary to do more than say something like, "Before we finish I'd like to tell you a story (or give you something to do between now and the next session)."

Metaphorical objects may be introduced into the treatment at any time, provided rapport is satisfactory. Their use is simply a way of representing issues, feelings, even people, in an indirect and relatively non-threatening way. Whenever an approach in which such issues, feelings, or people are represented directly is contraindicated or has been tried and has failed, an indirect approach of some sort may be used.

HYPNOSIS AND THE DELIVERY OF METAPHORS

Milton Erickson often combined the use of metaphor with hypnosis, and Lankton and Lankton (1983) describe in detail their understanding of how he did this. The Lanktons evidently consider it important to use hypnotic trance in offering metaphors to clients. Whether Erickson did is less clear; indeed the Lanktons' book opens with a personal communication from Erickson that reads, "I invent a new theory and a new approach for each individual." This presumably means that we should not be dogmatic about our use of therapeutic methods, but instead should be flexible and creative, and match our therapeutic interventions to the needs of our clients.

How often do those we treat by means of therapeutic metaphors need hypnosis? There is a lack of hard data with which to answer this question, but in some ways it is a nonquestion. This is because of the difficulty of defining precisely when a state of hypnosis begins and when a person's normal state of awareness ends.

Hypnosis is a state of focussed attention and altered awareness of one's surroundings. Most, if not all, methods of inducing trance, whether formal or informal, direct or indirect, involve focussing attention on certain things, or perhaps just one thing, to the exclusion of everything else. As the subject's trance gets "deeper" various "hypnotic phenomena" may appear or become demonstrable; for example, arm levitation, catalepsy, dissociation, amnesia, and positive and negative hallucinations.

The distinction between simple daydreaming and hypnotic trance is hard to make. According to the Lanktons (1983), ''Fixation of attention is itself a minimal alteration in consciousness and produces signs of light trance'' (p. 131). Presumably, therefore, the person whose attention is fixated while listening intently to a story or engrossed in a game is in a state of light trance. If a client's attention is riveted on a story told as a therapeutic metaphor the same applies. We thus have little choice as to whether we use hypnosis or not, at least when we tell our clients stories that grab their attention. This may not apply to brief anecdotes and analogies, however. Perhaps the question we really need to consider is whether we need to take specific steps to induce an hypnotic trance, other than simply telling our story using the guidelines set out earlier in this chapter.

To my knowledge, no controlled clinical trials have been carried out to compare the effectiveness of metaphors given after the induction of trance with those given without such an induction. What, then, does our clinical experience and that of others tell us? It seems clear that the use of metaphor can be an effective way of communicating information and ideas—especially the latter—when direct communication fails; the frequent use of metaphors in many people's everyday conversation attests to this. Moreover, most people using metaphors in the course of conversation make no conscious attempt to induce an hypnotic trance in those to whom they are speaking. This suggests that there is no general need to induce trance to deliver an effective metaphor. Yet in treating some clients hypnosis may be a useful adjunct; in the trance state some therapeutic processes, of which the use of metaphor is but one, may be facilitated.

As was mentioned in Chapter 1, we have been said to have two languages. Watzlawick (1978) describes them as follows:

> The one, in which for instance this sentence is itself expressed, is objective, definitional, cerebral, logical, analytic; it is the language of reason, of science, explanation, and interpretation, and therefore the language of most schools of psycho-

therapy. The other . . . is much more difficult to define—precisely because it is not the language of definition. We might call it the language of imagery, of metaphor, of *pars pro toto*, perhaps of symbols, but certainly of synthesis and totality, and not of analytical dissection. (pp. 14–15)

In the book from which the foregoing quotation is taken, *The Language of Change* (1978), Watzlawick suggests that, as a general rule, the second of his "two languages" is the more effective in the production of the kind of changes we aim to help people achieve during psychotherapy. He makes extensive use of the metaphor—which seems more and more to be a physiological fact—of the right and left brains and their different functions, referring to "our two brains."

Watzlawick distinguishes what he calls right- and left-hemisphere language patterns. According to Watzlawick we dream in right hemisphere language, and puns, paradoxes, poetry, aphorisms—especially that subgroup called chiasms—ambiguities, allusions and of course metaphors, are also understood (at least in their deeper meanings) in the right cerebral hemisphere. None of these forms of communication rely on the direct, digital, logical communication of ideas, which is the business of the left hemisphere (see Chapter 3).

Watzlawick (1978) believes that "second-order" change is what is required in many of the more intractable problems with which clients come to therapists. Second-order change (see Watzlawick, Weakland & Fisch, 1974) implies going beyond the simple application of logical measures (like trying harder) to something much less logical, like laughing at one's earlier attempts to try harder, or even employing a totally paradoxical approach (Barker, 1981a). It is in the right hemisphere, Watzlawick maintains, that the processes responsible for second-order change occur. To get into contact with the right hemisphere, the left hemisphere must be blocked. Watzlawick regards the left hemisphere as a sort of logical watchdog maintaining the individual's problem-solving systems along certain predetermined lines. When circumstances change, however, these may no longer be effective. Second-order change is then required.

If we accept what Watzlawick says it seems that hypnosis helps us gain access to the right hemisphere; indeed many hypnotherapists suggest, during therapy, that the conscious mind may wish to take a break and wonder what the unconscious mind will do, or what resources it will make available to the subject. This may perhaps be a metaphor for the respective roles of the left and right hemispheres—or maybe the concept of the right and left hemispheres is the metaphor!

Metaphors themselves are vehicles designed to promote second-order change; it may be that, combined with hypnosis, which also facilitates second-order change, they are more effective than when used in the normally alert state. Thus a combined approach may be helpful in the more difficult cases.

MULTIPLE EMBEDDED METAPHORS

Lankton and Lankton (1983) discuss the use of what they call "multiple embedded metaphors." This procedure, which Milton Erickson used usually in association with hypnosis, seems to be more effective than the straightforward metaphor, at least in treating some of the more complex clinical problems. It is also more difficult to carry out successfully; the beginner should probably become comfortable with the use of single metaphors, which of course may be delivered in a series, before advancing to the use of the multiple embedded variety.

The essence of the process of using multiple embedded metaphors may be represented by the diagram in Figure 2. As the diagram indicates, Erickson often started to tell a story and then broke off before he had completed it and went on to something else; he would then return and complete the story later. In the meantime other work would have been done to help the client obtain access to needed resources or in some way to deal constructively with conflicts or problems.

Stage 1 of this process is simply the induction of a state of hypnotic trance. This may be done in any one of a variety of ways; this technique should only be used by therapists trained in hypnosis, who will be skilled in various conversational and other methods of trance induction.

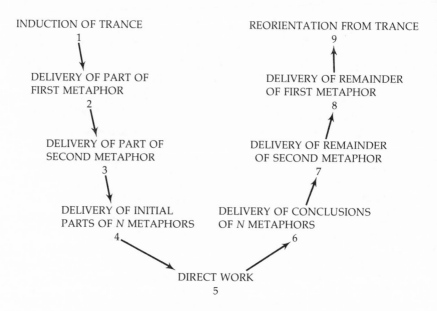

Figure 2. The multiple embedded metaphor process. (Adapted from Lankton & Lankton, 1983.)

In stage 2 a metaphor is offered that matches the situation which the client wishes to change. The end of this metaphor comes at stage 8, and often illustrates a desirable outcome, perhaps a surprising one or even a humorous one.

Stages 3 and 4 are parts of one process; stage 4, which may consist of one or more metaphors, may not be required at all—and indeed beginning therapists should keep it simple and not try and embed too many metaphors in one session. The stage 3 and 4 metaphors, with their endings in stages 6 and 7, are designed to help clients retrieve resources; they may be about people who found they had resources they were quite unaware of, similar to the self-esteem promoting metaphors described in Chapter 9. Stage 5, the direct work, may be any form of psychotherapeutic intervention one would normally use. The advantage of using such interventions in this situation is that clients will be more open to the input offered them, will be oriented to change, and will be expecting to learn how to use previously unused resources.

In stages 6 and 7 the metaphors started in stages 3 and 4 are completed, usually with material that suggests how the resources they refer to can be used in the situations in which they will be needed. In stage 7 the metaphor started in stage 2 is concluded with a happy ending, suggesting a desirable outcome.

This brief account of a complex process is intended to show that metaphors can be used, as they were by Erickson, as part of a larger, systematic treatment plan.

The embedding of metaphors in a therapy session can be done more simply, and even without the formal induction of trance. All you need do is start a story or task, break off in the middle to turn to something else, and complete the story later, having offered a number of other interventions in the meantime; these may be reframings, paradoxes, analogies, or other metaphors. The embedding of any sort of therapeutic intervention in the middle of a story that first defines a problem and then, in its concluding part, describes its resolution, seems to be a powerful treatment technique.

FACT OR FICTION?

Does it matter whether stories or anecdotes told as therapeutic metaphors are true or not? Probably not, or, at least in most cases, not much. The way a story is introduced should however take account of whether it is a true story or a fictional one. Most clients—all except the very young—realize that a fairy tale is fiction, so if a story is presented as a fairy tale there is usually no need to define it as fiction other than by saying that it is a fairy tale.

If a story is factual, it is usually easy to introduce it in a matter-of-fact way, saying, "This situation reminds me of . . . ," or "I'd like to tell you about an experience a friend of mine once had . . . ," or "I think you'll be interested in . . . ," or something of that sort. If a story is fictional, one may wish to say, "I once heard this story, but I'm not sure if it's true," or "This probably isn't true, but it's a fascinating tale you might be interested in hearing."

Whether there is any inherent therapeutic advantage in telling stories based on real characters as opposed to fictional ones is unclear. Sometimes, probably, allusions to real events and people can be more effective, especially when hypnotic trance is not induced. In trance the conscious mind does not seem to be as watchful or as critical of statements whose logic is questionable as when the subject is in the fully alert state. The anecdote about Jane Austen, offered earlier, might have more impact as a result of being true (as I believe it is), than it would if it were fictional.

ASSESSING FEEDBACK

An important part of the delivery of any form of psychotherapeutic intervention is the assessing of clients' feedback. In indirect forms of therapy, such as metaphor, this is particularly important; while the conscious mind may be attending to the apparent meaning, or superficial interest, of the story or task, the therapist intends that the unconscious mind will be responding to the deeper, metaphorical meaning. But because this *is* unconscious, we cannot expect to be given information about it in direct, logical, or "left-hemisphere" language. Instead we need means of assessing the unconscious responses.

Fortunately there are ways of obtaining information about unconscious processes. Most of the feedback that can give us information about what is going on in our clients' unconscious minds is nonverbal; and if we receive conflicting verbal and nonverbal messages, the nonverbal ones are usually the more reliable.

The first thing to be noted is the *attention* being given the metaphor. Are the clients interested in what is being told them, or has the focus of their attention wandered elsewhere? The fact that clients appear not to be attending does not necessarily mean that, at the unconscious level, they are not hearing anything that is being said. But if their interest is clearly somewhere else, the response to the metaphor is usually poor. One of the advantages of hypnosis, incidentally, is the focusing of attention that it brings about.

The next thing to be noted is whether there is any *change in nonverbal information* as the different parts of the metaphor are offered to the clients. In assessing nonverbal responses, change is our best indicator that messages are being received by clients and that some unconscious response is occurring.

Precisely which nonverbal responses will be useful will vary from client to client. It is a good plan to observe clients carefully from one's first contact with them in order to become familiar with their styles of nonverbal communication. The following is Erickson's description of this process:

> The senior author [Erickson] prefers to utilize a patient's own natural means of ideomotor signaling whenever possible. Whatever natural and automatic movements a patient makes in ordinary conversation can be studied for their metacommunicative value. Besides the more obvious head and hand movements, eye-blinking (slow or rapid), body-shifting, leg movements, arm position (e.g. crossed over one another as a "defense") lip-wetting, swallowing, and facial cues, such as frowning and tensions around the mouth and jaw, can be studied for their commentary on what is being said verbally. (Erickson & Rossi, 1981, p. 122)

Finally, of course, we must always be alert for changes in clients' behaviors. Therapy is intended to produce changes in how our clients behave, which in turn reflects how they feel and how they understand their world. It is the changes in clients' behaviors that are the "bottom line" of therapy.

SUMMARY

The effective delivery of therapeutic metaphors requires that rapport first be firmly established between therapist and client. Metaphors are best delivered within a context in which stories, tasks, and the use of analogies, similes, and allusions to other subjects have been regular features of the therapy interviews.

Stories and other metaphors should be carefully planned and introduced as things that may intrigue, interest, or challenge the clients, and should usually be offered quite casually, in a permissive rather than an authoritarian manner. It may be an advantage, in some cases, to offer them after first inducing a state of hypnotic trance, but they can be effective without doing this. Careful attention to the responses offered by clients, especially the nonverbal or "ideomotor" ones, is important.

A PRACTICAL EXERCISE

Select a case, the clinical details of which you are familiar with, from your current caseload; this may be a single client, a family, or a marital couple. Devise a full-length metaphorical story, using the principles that were used in developing the metaphor for Harold's and Jane's family in Chapter 3. As you work on making your story isomorphic with the situation of your client or clients, you may find it helpful to review also the story of Brett and Corinne, and the explanation of how this could be used metaphorically, in Chapter 9.

When you have completed your story, write or type it out in full, or dictate it and have it typed. Then practice delivering it, as set out in this chapter, either to a colleague who is familiar with your work, or to a tape recorder so that you can review it later. Discussing it critically with a colleague who has also studied this book, or who is familiar with the use of metaphorical methods, will be particularly useful.

At the end of this process you will have available a therapeutic metaphor that you can, if you wish and if conditions indicate, deliver to clients, using the techniques set out in this chapter.

Epilogue

Human communication is a complex process. When, as psychotherapists, we accept people for treatment, we commit ourselves to getting involved in the complexities of that communication process.

The focus in this book has been on one particular type of communication—communication by metaphor. Metaphorical devices can never be more than one of the tools of our trade. I recall the visit of an electrician who came to my home to do some work on the rather antiquated wiring system in our 50-year-old residence. He carried a box of tools and he also wore a hefty belt with loops, in which were inserted an impressive variety of screwdrivers, pliers, devices for testing circuits and other assorted tools. Like that electrician, therapists today must have a wide variety of tools readily available to them in order to be able to tackle the many and various problems that may present themselves.

Like electricians we must not only possess many tools, but also be skilled in using them all; and we need to know which tool to use in each of the many clinical situations we may encounter in our day-to-day work. And of course the ability to use metaphors effectively in our work is just one of the tools that need to hang from our therapeutic belts.

A book on therapeutic metaphors can never be more than a guide and a means of inspiring its readers to try some therapeutic approaches they may not have used previously. This volume has presented examples and ideas which I hope you will adapt for your own use. The human dilemmas with which people come to us are too varied and complex for the "cookbook" approach to be applicable, and I have tried hard to avoid writing a cookbook. I hope, rather, that the book will be a starting point from which you will develop your own unique and personal ways of using metaphor. In using this guide, though, or when any other sophisticated therapeutic device is used, attention to detail is important—just as it is in dealing with electrical circuits and devices, which can be very dangerous if they are not properly installed and serviced.

In our work as therapists the details are the words and the nonverbal communications we use. Choosing the right words is as important as choosing suitable metaphors. It is often better to talk of challenges than of problems, of construction companies than of demolition companies, of resources than of handicaps, of the future than of the past. Stories and tasks with a happy outcome are not only more fun, they tend to be more effective too. In this book we have talked about building a garden shed, about finding a new use for an old tractor, about discovering how to train a recalcitrant puppy and, in Chapter 7, about how everything has a bright side, something that all of us—but perhaps especially our clients—need to know.

A final word about the "unconscious." I have used this term to describe that part of us in which are stored all the information and the many "learnings" we have acquired throughout our lives. This use of the term—which differs from that in traditional psychoanalysis—emphasizes the role of the unconscious as a resource rather than as the seat of unresolved conflicts and other problems.

To the Ericksonian therapist the unconscious comprises everything we know but do not know we know, as well as all the psychological resources we possess but of which we are currently unaware. When we say that something is "unconscious," we refer to the extent to which we are consciously aware of it; we do not imply that it is deeply repressed, so that perhaps only prolonged psychoanalysis could enable us to have access to it. It is with this part of our clients' minds—perhaps corresponding more to Freud's "preconscious" than to what he meant by the "unconscious"—that we aim to communicate when we use therapeutic metaphors and other strategic therapy devices.

References

American Psychiatric Association (1980). *Diagnostic and Statistical Manual III.* Washington, D.C.: American Psychiatric Association.

Angelo, C. (1981). The use of the metaphoric object in family therapy. *American Journal of Family Therapy, 9,* 69–78.

Anthony, E. J. (1957). An experimental approach to the psychopathology of childhood: Encopresis. *British Journal of Medical Psychology, 30,* 146–75.

Bandler, R., & Grinder, J. (1979). *Frogs Into Princes.* Moab, Utah: Real People Press.

Bandler, R., Grinder, J., & Satir, V. (1976). *Changing With Families.* Palo Alto: Science and Behavior Books.

Barker, P. (1978). The "impossible" child—Some approaches to treatment. *Canadian Journal of Psychiatry, 23,* special supplement, SS1–21.

Barker, P. (1981a). Paradoxical techniques in psychotherapy. In D. S. Freeman & B. Trute (Eds.), *Treating Families With Special Needs.* Ottawa: Canadian Association of Social Workers.

Barker, P. (1981b). *Basic Family Therapy.* London: Granada, and Baltimore: University Park Press.

Barker, P. (1983). *Basic Child Psychiatry* (4th ed.). London: Granada, and Baltimore: University Park Press.

Barnhill, L. H., & Longo, D. (1978). Fixation and regression in the family life cycle. *Family Process, 17,* 469–78.

Bettelheim, B. (1977). *The Uses of Enchantment.* New York: Vintage Books.

Blum, K. (1984). *Handbook of Abusable Drugs.* New York: Gardner Press.

Chaplin, C. (1964). *My Autobiography.* London: The Bodley Head.

Coppersmith, E. I. (1981). Developmental reframing. *Journal of Strategic and Systemic Therapies, 1,* 1–8.

Coppersmith, E. I. (1983). From "hyperactive" to "normal but naughty": A multisystem partnership in delabeling. *International Journal of Family Psychiatry, 3,* 131–44.

Coppersmith, E. I. (1985). "We've got a secret!": A non-marital marital therapy. In A. S. Gurman (Ed.), *Casebook of Marital Therapy.* New York: Guilford.

Coppersmith, E. I. (forthcoming). In M. Karpel (Ed.), *Family Resources*. New York: Guilford.

Crowley, R., & Mills, J. (1984). *The multisensory metaphor: Innovative dissociative techniques for children* and *Interrupting adult psychosomatic symptomatology: An integration of right-brain phenomena and multisensory metaphors*. Papers presented at the 1984 American Society of Clinical Hypnosis Scientific Meeting Symposium XI, entitled Neurolinguistics and Metaphors: Innovative Hypnotherapy.

Crowley, R., & Mills, J. (1986, in press). *Therapeutic Metaphors for Children and the Child Within*. New York: Brunner/Mazel.

Dance, S. (1974). *The World of Swing*. New York: Charles Scribner's Sons.

Dilts, R., Grinder, J., Bandler, R., Bandler, L. C., & DeLozier, J. (1980). *Neuro-Linguistic Programming: Volume I*. Cupertino, California: Meta Publications.

Duvall, E. M. (1977). *Marriage and Family Development* (5th ed.). Philadelphia: Lippincott.

Epstein, N. B., Bishop, D. S., & Levin, S. (1978). The McMaster model of family functioning. *Journal of Marriage and Family Counselling, 4*, 19–31.

Erickson, M. H. (1980a). *The Nature of Hypnosis and Suggestion. (Collected Papers*, Vol. I, E. L. Rossi, Ed.). New York: Irvington.

Erickson, M. H. (1980b). *Hypnotic Alteration of Sensory, Perceptual and Psychological Processes. (Collected Papers*, Vol. II, E. L. Rossi, Ed.). New York: Irvington.

Erickson, M. H. (1980c). *Hypnotic Investigation of Psychodynamic Processes. (Collected Papers*, Vol. III, E. L. Rossi, Ed.). New York: Irvington.

Erickson, M. H. (1980d). *Innovative Psychotherapy. (Collected Papers*, Vol. IV, E. L. Rossi, Ed.). New York: Irvington.

Erickson, M. H. (1980e). *A Teaching Seminar With Milton H. Erickson, M.D.* New York: Brunner/Mazel.

Erickson, M. H., Hershman, S., & Secter, I. I. (1961). *The Practical Application of Medical and Dental Hypnosis*. Chicago: Seminars on Hypnosis Publishing Co.

Erickson, M. H., Rossi, E. L., & Rossi, S. I. (1976). *Hypnotic Realities*. New York: Irvington.

Erickson, M. H., & Rossi, E. L. (1981). *Experiencing Hypnosis: Therapeutic Approaches to Altered States*. New York: Irvington.

Ferris, T. (1980). Hopeful prophet who speaks for human aspirations. (An interview with Lewis Thomas.) *Smithsonian, 11*, 1, 127–42.

Frankl, V. (1962). *Man's Search for Meaning: An Introduction to Logotherapy*. Boston: Beacon Press.

Good News Bible (1976). American Bible Society.

Gordon, D. (1978). *Therapeutic Metaphors*. Cupertino, California: Meta Publications.

Gross, G. (1979). The family angel—The scapegoat's counterpart. *Family Therapy, 6*, 133–6.

Haley, J. (1973). *Uncommon Therapy: The Psychiatric Techniques of Milton H. Erickson, M.D.* New York: Norton.

Haley, J. (1976). *Problem-Solving Therapy*. San Francisco: Jossey-Bass.

Haley, J. (1984). *Ordeal Therapy*. San Francisco: Jossey-Bass.

Hammond, C. D. (1984). Myths about Erickson and Ericksonian Hypnosis. *American Journal of Clinical Hypnosis, 26*, 236–45.

Hanks, P. (Ed.) (1979). *Collins Dictionary of the English Language*. London: Collins.

Jones, M., & Chilton, J. (1971). *Louis*. London: Studio Vista.

Lamb, S. P. (1980). *Hemispheric Specialization and Storytelling*. Thesis for Master of Arts in Folklore and Mythology. University of California, Los Angeles.

Lankton, S., & Lankton, C. (1983). *The Answer Within*. New York: Brunner/ Mazel.

Lines, K. (1970). *Dick Whittington Retold*. London: The Bodley Head.

Madanes, C. (1981). *Strategic Family Therapy*. San Francisco: Jossey-Bass.

Minuchin, S. (1974). *Families and Family Therapy*. Cambridge, Massachusetts: Harvard University Press.

Oliver, P. (1963). *Blues Fell This Morning*. London: Jazz Book Club/Cassell.

Ornstein, R. (1978). The split brain and the whole. *Human Nature, 1*, 76–83.

Orwell, G. (1945). *Animal Farm: A Fairy Story*. London: Secker and Warburg.

Palazzoli, S. M., Boscolo, L. G., Cecchin, G. F., & Prata, G. (1974). The treatment of children through brief treatment of their parents. *Family Process, 13*, 429–42.

Papp, P. (1980). The use of fantasy in a couples group. In M. Andolfi & I. Zwerling (Eds.), *Dimensions of Family Therapy*. New York: Guilford Press.

Papp, P. (1982). Staging reciprocal metaphors in a couples group. *Family Process, 21*, 453–467.

Rae-Grant, N. I. (1978). Arresting the vicious cycle—Care and treatment of adolescents displaying the Ovinnik syndrome. *Canadian Journal of Psychiatry, 23*, special supplement, SS22–40.

Robins, L. (1966). *Deviant Children Grown Up*. Baltimore: Williams and Wilkins.

Rogers, L., TenHouten, W., Kaplan, C. D., & Gardiner, M. (1977). Hemispheric specialization of bilingual Hopi Indian children. *International Journal of Neuroscience, 8*, 1–6.

Romig, D. A. (1978). *Justice For Our Children*. Lexington, Massachusetts: D.C. Heath.

Rosen, S. (Ed.) (1982). *My Voice Will Go With You: The Teaching Tales of Milton H. Erickson, M.D.* New York: Norton.

Rutter, M. (1973). Why are London school children so disturbed? *Proceedings of the Royal Society of Medicine, 66*, 1221–25.

Rutter, M., Tizard, J., & Whitmore, K. (1970). *Education, Health and Behaviour*. London: Longman.

Satir, V. (1967). *Conjoint Family Therapy*. Palo Alto: Science and Behavior Books.

Satir, V. (1972). *Peoplemaking*. Palo Alto: Science and Behavior Books.

Shamsie, S. J. (1981). Antisocial adolescents: Our treatments do not work—Where do we go from here? *Canadian Journal of Psychiatry, 26*, 357–64.

Stanley, L. (1980). Treatment of ritualistic behavior in an eight-year-old girl by response prevention. *Journal of Child Psychology and Psychiatry, 21*, 85–90.

Steffenhagen, R. A. (1983). *Hypnotic Techniques for Increasing Self-Esteem*. New York: Irvington.

Ten Boom, C. (1954). *A Prisoner and Yet . . .* Fort Washington, Pennsylvania: Christian Literature Publications.

Thomas, A., & Chess, S. (1977). *Temperament and Development*. New York: Brunner/Mazel.

Turbayne, C. M. (1970). *The Myth of Metaphor*. Columbia, South Carolina:

University of South Carolina Press.
van der Hart, O. (1983). *Rituals in Psychotherapy: Transition and Continuity*. New York: Irvington.
Wahler, R. G. (1976). Deviant child behavior within the family: Developmental speculations and behavior change strategies. In H. Leitenberg (Ed.), *Handbook of Behavior Modification and Therapy*. Englewood Cliffs, New Jersey: Prentice-Hall.
Warren, M. Q. (1978). The "impossible" child, the difficult child, and other assorted delinquents: Etiology, characteristics and incidence. *Canadian Journal of Psychiatry, 23*, special supplement, SS41–60.
Watzlawick, P. (1978). *The Language of Change*. New York: Basic Books.
Watzlawick, P., Beavin, J. H., & Jackson, D. D. (1967). *Pragmatics of Human Communication*. New York: Norton.
Watzlawick, P., Weakland, J., & Fisch, R. (1974). *Change: Principles of Problem Formation and Problem Resolution*. New York: Norton.
Zeig, J. (1980). In M. H. Erickson, *A Teaching Seminar With Milton H. Erickson, M.D.* New York: Brunner/Mazel.

Author Index

Subject Index

219